Language Arts 500
Teacher's Guide

P9-CRI-146

CONTENTS

Author: **Alpha Omega Publications**

Editor: Alan Christopherson, M.S.

Alpha Omega Publications ®

300 North McKemy Avenue, Chandler, Arizona 85226-2618

CURRICULUM

OVERVIEW

LANGUAGE ARTS

Curriculum Overview
Grades K–12

Kindergarten

Language Arts Lessons

1-40	41-80	81-120	121-160
Alphabet-say the alphabet **Colors-**recognize colors **Directions-**left to right **Following directions-**given once **Grammar-**form simple sentences **Listening skills** **Personal recognition-**read and write first name -know age and address -recognize names of family members **Phonics-**short *a, e, i* vowels -initial: *b, t, m, r, s, n, d, p, l* -form and read simple words -form rhyming words **Shapes-**circle, square, triangle, and rectangle -recognize shapes in objects **Stories and Poems-**create simple stories and poems **Writing-**form circle and lines -*Aa, Bb, Dd, Ee, Ii, Ll, Mm, Nn, Pp, Rr, Ss,* and *Tt*	**Grammar-**sentences begin with capital, end with period **Patterns-**simple shape, color patterns **Personal recognition-**read and write first and last name **Phonics-**short *a, e, i, o, and u* vowels -initial: *k, c, ck, f, h, g, j, v, w, y, z, qu, and x* -read simple sentences **Position/direction concepts-**in/out, in front of/behind, up/down, on/off, open/closed, over/under **Sequencing-**alphabetical order -simple story **Shapes-**oval **Size concepts-**big/little, large/small **Writing-***Kk, Cc, Ff, Hh, Oo, Gg, Jj, Vv, Ww, Uu, Yy, Zz, Qq,* and *Xx*	**Phonics-**recognize the short vowel sounds -recognize all initial consonant sounds -recognize long *a, e, i, o,* and *u* sounds -silent *e* -initial consonant digraphs: *sh, ch,* both soft and hard *th* -final consonant sounds: *_b, _ck, _k, _l* **Word recognition-**color words, number words & shape words **Writing-**name -complete alphabet, capital and small letters -all color words -number words: *one, two, three, four, five, six* -shape words: *circle, square, triangle*	**Phonics-**recognize the long vowel sounds -initial consonant diagraphs: *wh;* review *ch, sh, th* -recognize all final consonant sounds: **Stories and poems-**create, tell, and recite stories and poems **Word recognition-**position/direction words: *up/down, high/low, in, inside, out, outside, top/bottom* -number words: *seven, eight, nine, ten* -shape words: *rectangle, oval, star* **Writing-**number words: *seven, eight, nine, ten* -shape words: *rectangle, oval, star* -position/direction words: *up/down, high/low, in, inside, out, outside, top/bottom*

	Grade 1	Grade 2	Grade 3
LIFEPAC 1	**FUN WITH PHONICS** • Short vowel sounds • Consonants • Main ideas • Rhyming words	**FROM SOUNDS TO WORDS** • Talk • Write • Our alphabet • Vowels • Consonants	**OLD AND NEW SKILLS** • Vowels • Consonants • Sentence phrases • Capital letters • Reading skills
LIFEPAC 2	**FUN WITH PHONICS** • Kinds of sentences • Cardinal • Ordinal numbers • Suffixes • Plurals • Classifying	**WORDS TO SENTENCES** • Letters in words • Words in phrases • Words in sentences • Reading comprehension	**BUILDING WORDS SENTENCES** • Vowels - long, short • Questions • ABC order • Capital letters
LIFEPAC 3	**FUN WITH PHONICS** • Consonant digraphs • Compounds • Syllables • Possessives • Contractions • Soft c and g	**HOW THE SENTENCE BEGINS** • Sentences to talk • Sentences to write • Capital letters • Consonant blends	**WORDS • GETTING TO THE ROOTS** • Root words • Dictionary guide words • Synonyms • Antonyms • Capital letters
LIFEPAC 4	**FUN WITH PHONICS** • Paragraphs • Silent letters • Sequencing • Subject-verb agreement	**A SECOND LOOK AT LETTERS** • Capital letters • Consonant blends • Long vowels • Short vowels	**WORDS • HOW TO USE THEM** • Noun • Verb • Adjective •Adverb • Irregular vowels • Composition
LIFEPAC 5	**FUN WITH PHONICS** • Long vowels • Homonyms • Poetry • Syllables • Possessives • Contractions • Plurals • Suffixes	**SENTENCE START TO FINISH** • Ending punctuation • Capital letters • Digraphs • Creative writing	**SENTENCE • START TO FINISH** • Question marks • Commas • Periods • Paragraphs • Plural words
LIFEPAC 6	**FUN WITH PHONICS** • R-controlled vowels • Writing stories • Pronouns • Following directions	**MORE ABOUT PUNCTUATION** • Contractions • Digraphs • Vowel sounds • Dictionary • ABC order	**ALL ABOUT BOOKS** • Books • Stories • Poems • Card catalogue • Critical thinking
LIFEPAC 7	**FUN WITH PHONICS** • Vowel digraphs • Letters - business, friendly, invitations • Syllables	**WORDS • GETTING TO THE ROOTS** • Root words • Suffixes • Creative writing • More about the dictionary	**READING AND WRITING** • For directions • Friendly letters • Pronouns • Fact • Fiction
LIFEPAC 8	**FUN WITH PHONICS** • Vowel digraphs • Subject-verb agreement • Compounds • Contractions • Possessives •Pronouns	**WORDS • BEGINNING & ENDING** • Prefixes • Suffixes • Cursive handwriting • Creative writing • Dictionary	**READING SKILLS** • For sequence • For detail • Verbs - being, compound • Drama
LIFEPAC 9	**FUN WITH PHONICS** • Vowel digraphs • Titles • Main ideas • Sentences • Paragraphs • Proper nouns	**WORDS • HOW TO USE THEM** • Verbs - singular, plural • Verb tense • Creative writing • Dictionary	**MORE READING & WRITING** • For information • Thank you letters • Book reports • Reference books
LIFEPAC 10	**LOOKING BACK** • Letters and sounds • Contractions • Plurals • Possessives • Sentences • Stories	**LOOKING BACK** • Vowels • Consonants • Contractions • Compounds • Sentences • Phrases • Dictionary	**LOOKING BACK** • Reading for comprehension • Sentence punctuation • Writing letters • Parts of Speech

Grade 4	Grade 5	Grade 6	
WRITTEN COMMUNICATION • Word derivations • Story sequence • Writing an outline • Writing a report	STORY MESSAGES • Main idea • Plot • Character • Setting • Dialogue • Diphthong • Digraph	READING FOR A PURPOSE • Critical thinking • Research data • Parables • Synonyms	LIFEPAC 1
SOUNDS TO WORDS • Hard and soft – c and g • Parts of dictionary • Accented syllables • Haiku Poetry	MAIN IDEAS • Poetry • Story • Synonyms • Compounds • Topic sentence • Adjectives • Nouns	FORMING NEW WORDS • Prefixes • Suffixes • Synonyms • Antonyms • Adjectives • Adverbs • Critical thinking	LIFEPAC 2
WORDS • HOW TO USE THEM • Prefixes • Suffixes • Homonyms • Antonyms • Poetry • Stories • Writing an outline	WORDS TO STORIES • Subject • Predicate • Adverbs • Idioms • Critical thinking • Writing a short story	BETTER READING • Story elements • Author's purpose • Information sources • Outline	LIFEPAC 3
MORE WORDS • HOW TO USE THEM • Parts of speech • Possession • Written directions • Verb tenses	WRITTEN REPORT • Outline • Four types of sentences • Metaphor • Simile • Writing the report	SENTENCES • Capitals • Punctuation • Four types of sentences • Author's purpose • Propaganda	LIFEPAC 4
WRITING FOR CLARITY • Figures of speech • Capital letters • Punctuation marks • Writing stories	STORY ELEMENTS • Legend • Implied meaning • Dialogue • Quotations • Word order • Usage • Critical thinking	READING SKILLS • Following directions • Literary forms • Phrases • Nouns • Verbs • Paragraph structure	LIFEPAC 5
FUN WITH FICTION • Book reports • Fiction • Nonfiction • Parables • Fables • Poetry	POETRY • Rhythm • Stanza • Symbolism • Personification • Irregular plurals	POETRY • Similes • Metaphors • Alliteration • Homonyms • Palindromes • Acronyms • Figures of speech	LIFEPAC 6
FACT AND FICTION • Nouns • Verbs • Contractions • Biography • Fables • Tall Tales	WORD USAGE • Nouns - common, plural, possessive • Fact • Opinion • Story • Main idea	STORIES • Story elements • Nouns • Pronouns • Vowel digraphs • Business letter	LIFEPAC 7
GRAMMAR AND WRITING • Adjectives to compare • Adverbs • Figurative language • Paragraphs	ALL ABOUT VERBS • Tense • Action • Participles • Of being • Regular • Irregular • Singular • Plural	NEWSPAPERS • Propaganda • News stories • Verbs – auxiliary, tenses • Adverbs	LIFEPAC 8
THE WRITTEN REPORT • Planning a report • Finding information • Outline • Writing a report	READING FLUENCY • Speed reading • Graphic aids • Study skills • Literary forms	READING THE BIBLE • Parables • Proverbs • Hebrew - poetry, prophecy • Bible history • Old Testament law	LIFEPAC 9
LOOKING BACK • Reading skills • Nouns • Adverbs • Written communication • Literary forms	LOOKING BACK • Literary forms • Parts of speech • Writing skills • Study skills	LOOKING BACK • Literary forms • Writing letters • Parts of speech • Punctuation	LIFEPAC 10

Language Arts LIFEPAC Overview

	Grade 7	Grade 8	Grade 9
LIFEPAC 1	**WORD USAGE** • Nouns – proper, common • Pronouns • Prefixes • Suffixes • Synonyms • Antonyms	**IMPROVE COMMUNICATION** • Roots • Inflections • Affixes • Interjections • Directions – oral, written • Non-verbal communication	**STRUCTURE OF LANGUAGE** • Nouns • Adjectives • Verbs • Prepositions • Adverbs • Conjunctions • Sentence parts

LIFEPAC 2	**MORE WORD USAGE**
	• Speech – stress, pitch
	• Verbs – tenses
	• Principle parts
	• Story telling
		ALL ABOUT ENGLISH
		• Origin of language
		• Classification–
		   nouns, pronouns, verbs,
		   adjectives, adverbs
			NATURE OF LANGUAGE
			• Origin of language
			• Use – oral and written
			• Dictionary
			• Writing a paper

LIFEPAC 3	**BIOGRAPHIES** • Biography as a form • Flashback technique • Deductive reasoning • Words – base, root	**PUNCTUATION AND WRITING** • Connecting and interrupting • The Essay • Thesis Statement	**PRACTICAL ENGLISH** • Dictionary use • Mnemonics • Writing a paper • Five minute speech
LIFEPAC 4	**LANGUAGE STRUCTURE** • Verbs – tenses • Principle parts • Sentence creativity • Speech – pitch, accent	**WORDS • HOW TO USE THEM** • Dictionary • Thesaurus • Accent • Diacritical mark • Standard • Nonstandard	**SHORT STORY FUNDAMENTALS** • Plot • Setting • Characterization • Conflict • Symbolism
LIFEPAC 5	**NATURE OF ENGLISH** • Formal • Informal • Redundant expressions • Verb tenses • Subject–verb agreement	**CORRECT LANGUAGE** • Using good form • Synonyms • Antonyms • Homonyms • Good speaking qualities	**LANGUAGE IN LITERATURE** • Collective Nouns • Verbs • Use of comparisons • Gerunds • Participles • Literary genres

LIFEPAC 6	**MECHANICS OF ENGLISH**
	• Punctuation
	• Complements • Modifiers
	• Clauses – subordinate,
	  coordinate
		LANGUAGE AND LITERATURE
		• History of English
		• Coordination and
		  subordination
		• Autobiography
			ENHANCED READING SKILLS
			• Author's message
			• Using Visual Aids –
			  charts, graphs, tables
			• Understanding poetry

LIFEPAC 7	**THE NOVEL**
	• The Hiding Place
	• Sequence of events
	• Author's purpose
	• Character sketch
		CRITICAL THINKING
		• Word evaluation
		• The Paragraph –
		  structure, coherence,
		  introductory, concluding
			COMMUNICATION
			• Planning a speech
			• Listening comprehension
			• Letters – business,
			  informal, social

LIFEPAC 8	**LITERATURE** • Nonfiction • Listening skills • Commas • Semicolons • Nonverbal communications	**WRITE • LISTEN • READ** • Business letters • Personal letters • Four steps to listen • Nonfiction	**LIBRARY AND DRAMA** • Library resources • Drama – history, elements, reading • The Miracle Worker
LIFEPAC 9	**COMPOSITIONS** • Sentence types • Quality of paragraph • Pronunciation • Nonsense literature	**SPEAK AND WRITE** • Etymology • Modifiers • Person • Number • Tense • Oral report	**STUDIES IN THE NOVEL** • History • Define • Write • Critical essay • Twenty Thousand Leagues Under the Sea
LIFEPAC 10	**LOOKING BACK** • Parts of speech • Sentence structure • Punctuation • How to communicate	**LOOKING BACK** • Composition structure • Parts of speech • Critical thinking • Literary forms	**LOOKING BACK** • Communication – writing speaking, listening • Using resources • Literature review

Grade 10	Grade 11	Grade 12	
EVOLUTION OF ENGLISH • Historical development • Varieties of English • Substandard & standard • Changes in English	ENGLISH USES • VARIETIES • Standard • Nonstandard • Professional • Literary • Lexicography – purpose, bibliography	THE WORTH OF WORDS • Word categories • Expository writing • Sentence structure • Diction	LIFEPAC 1
LISTENING AND SPEAKING • Noun plurals • Suffixes • Creating a speech • Nature of listening	EFFECTIVE SENTENCES • Subordinate – clauses, conjunctions • Relative pronouns • Verbals • Appositives	STRUCTURE OF LANGUAGE • Parts of speech • Sentence structure • Subordinate phrases • Subordinate clauses	LIFEPAC 2

EFFECTIVE SENTENCES
• Participles • Infinitives
• Prepositions • Gerunds
• Sentences – simple,
  compound, complex
	SENTENCE WORKSHOP
	• Pronouns – personal,
	  reference, agreement
	• Misplaced modifiers
	• Parallel structure
		READ, RESEARCH, LISTEN
		• Reading skills
		• Resources for research
		• Taking notes
		• Drawing conclusions
			LIFEPAC 3

POWER OF WORDS • Etymology • Connotations • Poetic devices • Poetry – literal, figurative, symbolic	WHY STUDY READING? • Greek and Latin roots • Diacritical markings • Finding the main idea • Analyzing a textbook	GIFT OF LANGUAGE • Origin–Biblical, • Koine Greek • Purpose of Grammar • Semantics	LIFEPAC 4
ELEMENTS OF COMPOSITION • Paragraphs • Connectives • Transitions • Expository writing – elements, ideas	POETRY • Metrical feet • Sets • Musical effects • Universality • Imagery • Connotation	ENGLISH LITERATURE • Early England • Medieval England • Fourteenth century • Chaucer	LIFEPAC 5

STRUCTURE AND READING
• Subordinate clauses
• Pronouns – gender,
  case, agreement
• Reading for recognition
	NONFICTION
	• Elements
	• Types – essays, diaries,
	  newspaper, biography
	• Composition
		ELIZABETHAN LITERATURE
		• Poetry
		• Prose
		• Drama
		• Essay
			LIFEPAC 6

ORAL READING AND DRAMA • Skills of oral reading • Drama – history, irony elements, allegory • Everyman	AMERICAN DRAMA • Development • History • Structure • Purpose • Our Town	17TH—18TH CENTURY LITERATURE • Historical background • Puritan literature • Common sense – satire • Sensibility	LIFEPAC 7
THE SHORT STORY • Elements • Enjoying • Writing • The Literary Critique	AMERICAN NOVEL • Eighteenth, nineteenth twentieth century • The Old Man and the Sea • The Critical Essay	WRITING • SHORT STORY, POETRY • Fundamentals • Inspiration • Technique and style • Form and process	LIFEPAC 8
THE NOVEL • Elements • In His Steps • The Critical Essay • The Book Review	COMPOSITION • Stating the thesis • Research • Outline • Writing the paper	POETRY • ROMANTIC , VICTORIAN • Wordsworth • Coleridge • Gordon • Byron • Shelley • Keats • Tennyson • Hopkins • Robert and Elizabeth B Browning	LIFEPAC 9

LOOKING BACK
• Writing skills
• Speech skills
• Poetry • Drama
• Short stories • Novel
	LOOKING BACK
	• Analyzing written word
	• Effective sentences
	• Expository prose
	• Genres of American literature
		LOOKING BACK
		• Creative writing
		• English literature –
		  Medieval to
		  Victorian
			LIFEPAC 10

MANAGEMENT

STRUCTURE OF THE LIFEPAC CURRICULUM

The LIFEPAC curriculum is conveniently structured to provide one teacher handbook containing teacher support material with answer keys and ten student worktexts for each subject at grade levels two through twelve. The worktext format of the LIFEPACs allows the student to read the textual information and complete workbook activities all in the same booklet. The easy to follow LIFEPAC numbering system lists the grade as the first number(s) and the last two digits as the number of the series. For example, the Language Arts LIFEPAC at the 6th grade level, 5th book in the series would be LA 605.

Each LIFEPAC is divided into 3 to 5 sections and begins with an introduction or overview of the booklet as well as a series of specific learning objectives to give a purpose to the study of the LIFEPAC. The introduction and objectives are followed by a vocabulary section which may be found at the beginning of each section at the lower levels, at the beginning of the LIFEPAC in the middle grades, or in the glossary at the high school level. Vocabulary words are used to develop word recognition and should not be confused with the spelling words introduced later in the LIFEPAC. The student should learn all vocabulary words before working the LIFEPAC sections to improve comprehension, retention, and reading skills.

Each activity or written assignment has a number for easy identification, such as 1.1. The first number corresponds to the LIFEPAC section and the number to the right of the decimal is the number of the activity.

Teacher checkpoints, which are essential to maintain quality learning, are found at various locations throughout the LIFEPAC. The teacher should check 1) neatness of work and penmanship, 2) quality of understanding (tested with a short oral quiz), 3) thoroughness of answers (complete sentences and paragraphs, correct spelling, etc.), 4) completion of activities (no blank spaces), and 5) accuracy of answers as compared to the answer key (all answers correct).

The self test questions are also number coded for easy reference. For example, 2.015 means that this is the 15th question in the self test of Section II. The first number corresponds to the LIFEPAC section, the zero indicates that it is a self test question, and the number to the right of the zero the question number.

The LIFEPAC test is packaged at the centerfold of each LIFEPAC. It should be removed and put aside before giving the booklet to the student for study.

Answer and test keys have the same numbering system as the LIFEPACs and appear at the back of this handbook. The student may be given access to the answer keys (not the test keys) under teacher supervision so that he can score his own work.

A thorough study of the Curriculum Overview by the teacher before instruction begins is essential to the success of the student. The teacher should become familiar with expected skill mastery and understand how these grade level skills fit into the overall skill development of the curriculum. The teacher should also preview the objectives that appear at the beginning of each LIFEPAC for additional preparation and planning.

TEST SCORING and GRADING

Answer keys and test keys give examples of correct answers. They convey the idea, but the student may use many ways to express a correct answer. The teacher should check for the essence of the answer, not for the exact wording. Many questions are high level and require thinking and creativity on the part of the student. Each answer should be scored based on whether or not the main idea written by the student matches the model example. "Any Order" or "Either Order" in a key indicates that no particular order is necessary to be correct.

Most self tests and LIFEPAC tests at the lower elementary levels are scored at 1 point per answer; however, the upper levels may have a point system awarding 2 to 5 points for various answers or questions. Further, the total test points will vary; they may not always equal 100 points. They may be 78, 85, 100, 105, etc.

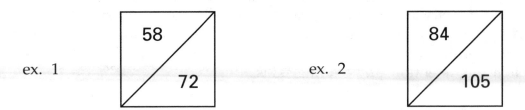

ex. 1   58 / 72   ex. 2   84 / 105

A score box similar to ex.1 above is located at the end of each self test and on the front of the LIFEPAC test. The bottom score, 72, represents the total number of points possible on the test. The upper score, 58, represents the number of points your student will need to receive an 80% or passing grade. If you wish to establish the exact percentage that your student has achieved, find the total points of his correct answers and divide it by the bottom number (in this case 72.) For example, if your student has a point total of 65, divide 65 by 72 for a grade of 90%. Referring to ex. 2, on a test with a total of 105 possible points, the student would have to receive a minimum of 84 correct points for an 80% or passing grade. If your student has received 93 points, simply divide the 93 by 105 for a percentage grade of 89%. Students who receive a score below 80% should review the LIFEPAC and retest using the appropriate Alternate Test found in the Teacher's Guide.

The following is a guideline to assign letter grades for completed LIFEPACs based on a maximum total score of 100 points.

LIFEPAC Test   =   60% of the Total Score (or percent grade)
Self Test   =   25% of the Total Score (average percent of self tests)
Reports   =   10% or 10* points per LIFEPAC
Oral Work   =   5% or 5* points per LIFEPAC
*Determined by the teacher's subjective evaluation of the student's daily work.

Example:

LIFEPAC Test Score	=	92%	92	x	.60	=	55 points
Self Test Average	=	90%	90	x	.25	=	23 points
Reports						=	8 points
Oral Work						=	4 points

TOTAL POINTS   =   90 points

Grade Scale based on point system:

100	–	94	=	A
93	–	86	=	B
85	–	77	=	C
76	–	70	=	D
Below		70	=	F

TEACHER HINTS and STUDYING TECHNIQUES

LIFEPAC Activities are written to check the level of understanding of the preceding text. The student may look back to the text as necessary to complete these activities; however, a student should never attempt to do the activities without reading (studying) the text first. Self tests and LIFEPAC tests are never open book tests.

Language arts activities (skill integration) often appear within other subject curriculum. The purpose is to give the student an opportunity to test his skill mastery outside of the context in which it was presented.

Writing complete answers (paragraphs) to some questions is an integral part of the LIFEPAC Curriculum in all subjects. This builds communication and organization skills, increases understanding and retention of ideas, and helps enforce good penmanship. Complete sentences should be encouraged for this type of activity. Obviously, single words or phrases do not meet the intent of the activity, since multiple lines are given for the response.

Review is essential to student success. Time invested in review where review is suggested will be time saved in correcting errors later. Self tests, unlike the section activities, are closed book. This procedure helps to identify weaknesses before they become too great to overcome. Certain objectives from self tests are cumulative and test previous sections; therefore, good preparation for a self test must include all material studied up to that testing point.

The following procedure checklist has been found to be successful in developing good study habits in the LIFEPAC curriculum.

1. Read the introduction and Table of Contents.
2. Read the objectives.
3. Recite and study the entire vocabulary (glossary) list.
4. Study each section as follows:
    a. Read the introduction and study the section objectives.
    b. Read all the text for the entire section, but answer none of the activities.
    c. Return to the beginning of the section and memorize each vocabulary word and definition.
    d. Reread the section, complete the activities, check the answers with the answer key, correct all errors, and have the teacher check.
    e. Read the self test but do not answer the questions.
    f. Go to the beginning of the first section and reread the text and answers to the activities up to the self test you have not yet done.
    g. Answer the questions to the self test without looking back.
    h. Have the self test checked by the teacher.
    i. Correct the self test and have the teacher check the corrections.
    j. Repeat steps a–i for each section.

5. Use the SQ3R* method to prepare for the LIFEPAC test.
6. Take the LIFEPAC test as a closed book test.
7. LIFEPAC tests are administered and scored under direct teacher supervision. Students who receive scores below 80% should review the LIFEPAC using the SQ3R* study method and take the Alternate Test located in the Teacher Handbook. The final test grade may be the grade on the Alternate Test or an average of the grades from the original LIFEPAC test and the Alternate Test.

   *SQ3R: Scan the whole LIFEPAC.
   Question yourself on the objectives.
   Read the whole LIFEPAC again.
   Recite through an oral examination.
   Review weak areas.

GOAL SETTING and SCHEDULES

Each school must develop its own schedule, because no single set of procedures will fit every situation. The following is an example of a daily schedule that includes the five LIFEPAC subjects as well as time slotted for special activities.

Possible Daily Schedule

8:15	–	8:25	Pledges, prayer, songs, devotions, etc.
8:25	–	9:10	Bible
9:10	–	9:55	Language Arts
9:55	–	10:15	Recess (juice break)
10:15	–	11:00	Mathematics
11:00	–	11:45	Social Studies
11:45	–	12:30	Lunch, recess, quiet time
12:30	–	1:15	Science
1:15	–		Drill, remedial work, enrichment*

*Enrichment: Computer time, physical education, field trips, fun reading, games and puzzles, family business, hobbies, resource persons, guests, crafts, creative work, electives, music appreciation, projects.

Basically, two factors need to be considered when assigning work to a student in the LIFEPAC curriculum.

The first is time. An average of 45 minutes should be devoted to each subject, each day. Remember, this is only an average. Because of extenuating circumstances a student may spend only 15 minutes on a subject one day and the next day spend 90 minutes on the same subject.

The second factor is the number of pages to be worked in each subject. A single LIFEPAC is designed to take 3 to 4 weeks to complete. Allowing about 3-4 days for LIFEPAC introduction, review, and tests, the student has approximately 15 days to complete the LIFEPAC pages. Simply take the number of pages in the LIFEPAC, divide it by 15 and you will have the number of pages that must be completed on a daily basis to keep the student on schedule. For example, a LIFEPAC containing 45 pages will require 3 completed pages per day. Again, this is only an average. While working a 45 page LIFEPAC, the student may complete only 1 page the first day if the text has a lot of activities or reports, but go on to complete 5 pages the next day.

Long range planning requires some organization. Because the traditional school year originates in the early fall of one year and continues to late spring of the following year, a calendar should be devised that covers this period of time. Approximate beginning and completion dates can be noted on the calendar as well as special occasions such as holidays, vacations and birthdays. Since each LIFEPAC takes 3-4 weeks or eighteen days to complete, it should take about 180 school days to finish a set of ten LIFEPACs. Starting at the beginning school date, mark off eighteen school days on the calendar and that will become the targeted completion date for the first LIFEPAC. Continue marking the calendar until you have established dates for the remaining nine LIFEPACs making adjustments for previously noted holidays and vacations. If all five subjects are being used, the ten established target dates should be the same for the LIFEPACs in each subject.

FORMS

The sample weekly lesson plan and student grading sheet forms are included in this section as teacher support materials and may be duplicated at the convenience of the teacher.

The student grading sheet is provided for those who desire to follow the suggested guidelines for assignment of letter grades found on page 3 of this section. The student's self test scores should be posted as percentage grades. When the LIFEPAC is completed the teacher should average the self test grades, multiply the average by .25 and post the points in the box marked self test points. The LIFEPAC percentage grade should be multiplied by .60 and posted. Next, the teacher should award and post points for written reports and oral work. A report may be any type of written work assigned to the student whether it is a LIFEPAC or additional learning activity. Oral work includes the student's ability to respond orally to questions which may or may not be related to LIFEPAC activities or any type of oral report assigned by the teacher. The points may then be totaled and a final grade entered along with the date that the LIFEPAC was completed.

The Student Record Book which was specifically designed for use with the Alpha Omega curriculum provides space to record weekly progress for one student over a nine week period as well as a place to post self test and LIFEPAC scores. The Student Record Books are available through the current Alpha Omega catalog; however, unlike the enclosed forms these books are not for duplication and should be purchased in sets of four to cover a full academic year.

WEEKLY LESSON PLANNER

Week of:

Monday	Subject	Subject	Subject	Subject

Tuesday	Subject	Subject	Subject	Subject

Wednesday	Subject	Subject	Subject	Subject

Thursday	Subject	Subject	Subject	Subject

Friday	Subject	Subject	Subject	Subject

WEEKLY LESSON PLANNER

Week of:

	Subject	Subject	Subject	Subject
Monday				
	Subject	Subject	Subject	Subject
Tuesday				
	Subject	Subject	Subject	Subject
Wednesday				
	Subject	Subject	Subject	Subject
Thursday				
	Subject	Subject	Subject	Subject
Friday				

Student Name _____   Year _____

Bible

LP #	Self Test Scores by Sections 1	2	3	4	5	Self Test Points	LIFEPAC Test	Oral Points	Report Points	Final Grade	Date
01											
02											
03											
04											
05											
06											
07											
08											
09											
10											

History & Geography

LP #	Self Test Scores by Sections 1	2	3	4	5	Self Test Points	LIFEPAC Test	Oral Points	Report Points	Final Grade	Date
01											
02											
03											
04											
05											
06											
07											
08											
09											
10											

Language Arts

LP #	Self Test Scores by Sections 1	2	3	4	5	Self Test Points.	LIFEPAC Test	Oral Points	Report Points	Final Grade	Date
01											
02											
03											
04											
05											
06											
07											
08											
09											
10											

Student Name _____   Year _____

Mathematics

LP #	Self Test Scores by Sections 1	2	3	4	5	Self Test Points.	LIFEPAC Test	Oral Points	Report Points	Final Grade	Date
01											
02											
03											
04											
05											
06											
07											
08											
09											
10											

Science

LP #	Self Test Scores by Sections 1	2	3	4	5	Self Test Points	LIFEPAC Test	Oral Points	Report Points	Final Grade	Date
01											
02											
03											
04											
05											
06											
07											
08											
09											
10											

Spelling/Electives

LP #	Self Test Scores by Sections 1	2	3	4	5	Self Test Points	LIFEPAC Test	Oral Points	Report Points	Final Grade	Date
01											
02											
03											
04											
05											
06											
07											
08											
09											
10											

NOTES

INSTRUCTIONS FOR LANGUAGE ARTS

The LIFEPAC curriculum from grades two through twelve is structured so that the daily instructional material is written directly into the LIFEPACs. The student is encouraged to read and follow this instructional material in order to develop independent study habits. The teacher should introduce the LIFEPAC to the student, set a required completion schedule, complete teacher checks, be available for questions regarding both content and procedures, administer and grade tests, and develop additional learning activities as desired. Teachers working with several students may schedule their time so that students are assigned to a quiet work activity when it is necessary to spend instructional time with one particular student.

Language arts includes those subjects that develop the students' communication skills. The LIFEPAC approach to combining reading, spelling, penmanship, composition, grammar, speech and literature in a single unit allows the teacher to integrate the study of these various language arts subject areas. The variety and scope of the curriculum may make it difficult for students to complete the required material within the suggested daily scheduled time of forty-five minutes. Spelling, book reports and various forms of composition may need to be completed during the afternoon enrichment period.

Cursive handwriting is introduced in the second grade LIFEPAC 208 with regular practice following in succeeding LIFEPACs. Diacritical markings are defined in the third grade LIFEPAC 304. A pronunciation key including diacritical markings is provided after the vocabulary word lists in all subjects beginning with LIFEPAC 305.

This section of the language arts Teacher's Guide includes the following teacher aids: Index of Concepts, Book *Report Form, Books Read Chart,* Suggested and Required Material (supplies), Additional Learning Activities, and LIFEPAC Spelling Tests.

The *Book Report Form* and the *Books Read Chart* may be duplicated for individual student use.

The Index of Concepts is a quick reference guide for the teacher who may be looking for a rule or explanation that applies to a particular concept. It does not identify each use of the concept in the various LIFEPACs. The concepts change by grade level with the emphasis on phonics and reading skills changing to spelling and grammar for the older students.

Spelling tests contained in the handbook are final spelling tests and should be administered with each Language Arts LIFEPAC test. Many words such as `piece' and `peace' are dependent on meaning for correct spelling. By placing the spelling words in sentences, the spelling tests simplify the teacher's work of properly presenting the correct words from the LIFEPAC spelling lists.

The materials section refers only to LIFEPAC materials and does not include materials which may be needed for the additional learning activities. Additional learning activities provide a change from the daily school routine, encourage the student's interest in learning and may be used as a reward for good study habits.

Concept	LIFEPAC	Section	Concept	LIFEPAC	Section
Abbreviations	503	3	limericks	506	2
			palindromes	506	2
Antonyms	503	3	puns	506	2
			novel	509	3
Composition			parable	508	2
dialogue	505	2	poetry		
note taking	504	3	couplet	506	3
outlining	504	3	diamante	502	3
paragraph	502	2	free verse	506	3
	503	3	humorous	506	2
personal reaction	507	1	inspirational	506	3
report	504	3	quatrain	506	3
	509	3	short story	509	3
sequence of events	505	2			
story	501	2	Literature (definition)	509	3
	505	3			
summary	503	2	Parts of Speech		
			adjectives	503	2
Compound Words	502	1	adverbs	503	2
				508	3
Dictionary Skills	501	2	articles	504	2
diacritical markings	510	2	nouns		
			irregular plurals	506	3
Handwriting	501	3	object of verb	507	2
	508	1	possessives	507	2
			proper/common	507	2
Heteronyms	503	1	singular/plural	507	2
			pronouns	507	2
Homonyms	503	3	verbs		
			action/being	508	1
Literary Forms			contraction	502	3
ballad	506	1,2		508	1
Bible literary forms	509	3	helping	508	1
drama	509	3	irregular	508	1
fable	508	2	participles	508	1
fiction/nonfiction	509	3		510	2
figurative language			singular/plural	508	1
idioms	503	3	tense	508	1
metaphor	506	3			
personification	506	3	Phonics/Spelling		
simile	506	3	(see Spelling/Handwriting pages)		
formal/informal English	502	3			
legend	505	1	Prefixes	503	2
literary devices				505	3
conundrums	506	2			

Concept	LIFEPAC	Section	Concept	LIFEPAC	Section
Propaganda	503	2			
Punctuation					
dialogue	505	2			
end of sentence	504	1			
Reading Skills	501	1			
author's purpose	503	3			
	510	2			
cause/effect	503	2			
comparison/contrast	510	3			
details	502	2			
	504	1			
fact/opinion	504	1			
graphic aids	509	2			
	510	3			
inference/implied meaning					
	504	1			
	507	3			
judging literature	505	1			
	507	3			
main idea	501	1			
	502	2			
sequence of events	503	1			
	507	1			
speed/fluency	509	1			
Root Words	503	2			
Sentence Structure					
kinds of sentences	504	1,2			
phrase	503	2			
	507	2			
sentence (definition)	503	1			
subject/predicate	504	2			
	507	2			
subject/verb agreement	508	1			
Suffixes	503	2			

BOOK REPORT FORM

Title _____   Your Name _____

Author _____   Date _____

Illustrator _____   Principal Characters _____

Number of Pages _____   _____

Copyright Date _____   _____

Fiction or Nonfiction _____   Setting _____

Summary: A summary gives the important events of a story or book. It skips most of the details but a few make the report more interesting. The summary should be written in complete sentences.

_____

_____

_____

_____

_____

_____

_____

_____

_____

_____

_____

_____

Tell why you did or did not like the book.

_____

_____

_____

_____

_____

_____

_____

_____

Name: _____

BOOKS READ

Title: Author: Date:	Title: Author: Date:	Title: Author: Date:	Title: Author: Date:
Title: Author: Date:	Title: Author: Date:	Title: Author: Date:	Title: Author: Date:
Title: Author: Date:	Title: Author: Date:	Title: Author: Date:	Title: Author: Date:
Title: Author: Date:	Title: Author: Date:	Title: Author: Date:	Title: Author: Date:
Title: Author: Date:	Title: Author: Date:	Title: Author: Date:	Title: Author: Date:
Title: Author: Date:	Title: Author: Date:	Title: Author: Date:	Title: Author: Date:
Title: Author: Date:	Title: Author: Date:	Title: Author: Date:	Title: Author: Date:
Title: Author: Date:	Title: Author: Date:	Title: Author: Date:	Title: Author: Date:
Title: Author: Date:	Title: Author: Date:	Title: Author: Date:	Title: Author: Date:

Materials Needed for LIFEPAC

Required: Suggested:
                                       Dictionary
                                       Red pencil

Additional Learning Activities

Section I

1. Discuss these questions.
   a. What is the importance of reading, listening, speaking, and writing correctly?
   b. Why are some students afraid of books?
   c. How can we become better thinkers?
   d. Why is it important to find the main idea of a paragraph, article, chapter, book, etc.?
   e. Why is it important to develop an adequate vocabulary?
   f. What do we mean by an author's style?
   g. What is dialogue?
   h. What are nouns?
   i. Why is it important to study a word, and how it is put together?
   j. What is a syllable?
   k. What is a vowel diphthong?
   l. Which are the common vowel diphthongs?
2. Read a passage into a tape recorder. Listen carefully as you replay the passage. Ask a friend to listen to the tape. Together decide what your good points are and how you can improve your oral reading.
3. Write a short paragraph. Have a friend decide what the main idea is.
4. Copy a full-page reading passage and list all the nouns and verbs. Rewrite the passage to change the ideas. The passage may be taken from a newspaper or a book.

Section II

1. Discuss these questions.
   a. Where were the students from the Christian School of the West going?
   b. What was the first place the group toured?
   c. What does *Anno Domini* mean?
   d. Where did Jesus go to worship and to read?
   e. What helps us know how to pronounce words correctly?
2. With a friend, make a puzzle using two common vowel-diphthong patterns.
3. Write a secret message to a friend. Use the diacritical marks and respellings from the dictionary for each word in the message.
4. Keep a personal glossary of new words you learn each day. List all your words in alphabetical order. Look up the definitions in the dictionary.

Section III

1. Discuss these questions.
    a. Who were the Scribes?
    b. What kind of skills are handwriting and spelling skills?
    c. Name some words that contain silent *e*.
2. Write your favorite memory verse in your best handwriting. Share it with a friend and let him give you any suggestions you might need for improving your handwriting.
3. With other students, have a spelling bee with your new list of spelling words.
4. Write a short story about kindness or forgiveness. State the main idea, characters, plot, and setting on a separate page. Your final copy should be written in your best handwriting.

Materials Needed for LIFEPAC

Required:

Suggested:
Dictionary
Encyclopedia

Additional Learning Activities

Section I

1. Discuss these questions.
    a. What are five skills that will help us receive information?
    b. What four skills will train us how to share our thinking with God and people?
    c. What is the Newberry Award?
    d. What are synonyms?
    e. What is a good way to organize material?
    f. Explain the difference between *fact* and *opinion*.
    g. What is a "gift of gab"?
    h. What do we mean by a compound word?
    i. When do we use hyphens in compound words?
    j. When does one use a hyphen when dividing words into syllables?
    k. What do we mean by consonant twins?
    l. Name the three most common ways to use a hyphen.
    m. How is a hyphen used at the end of the line?
2. Report on a favorite book. Include information about the author. Discuss with other students the author's authority.
3. Write a short story on something that you had to do that you feared (like Mafatu in the story "The Flight").

Section II

1. Discuss these questions.
    a. What do the main ideas in paragraphs tell you?
    b. What is the topic sentence?
    c. What is a summary sentence?
    d. What question can we ask to help us find the main idea?
    e. What kind of words help us focus on the author's main idea?
    f. How do we find specific information?
    g. What six questions can a detail answer?
    h. When do we develop courage?
    i. What kind of words does an author use to help him write detail sentences?
    j. What do we call descriptive words?
2. Write a paragraph that is similar to the one on courage in Section II of the LIFEPAC. Have a friend name the topic sentence and give a title to the paragraph.

3. Write a paragraph without using adjectives. Underline each noun. Have a friend add the adjectives. Discuss how the paragraph changed when the adjectives were added.

4. Using *who, what, when, where, why,* and *how,* write six questions about a topic of your choice. Locate the answers to your questions in an encyclopedia or resource book.

Section III

1. Discuss these questions.
    a. What kind of words help the author set the mood?
    b. Why are feelings important to us?
    c. What word do we use to discuss feelings?
    d. What are some mood words?
    e. What is diamond-shaped poetry?
    f. What are the two standard forms of the English language?
    g. When do we use formal English?
    h. When do we use informal English?
    i. What are contractions?
    j. How do contractions differ from compound words?

2. Write your feelings about different situations (examples: your feelings before taking a test, how you felt when you had a birthday party, etc.). Compare your feelings with a friend.

3. Write several "Diamante" poems and make an attractive booklet of your poems.

Materials Needed for LIFEPAC

Required:

Suggested:
Paper for handwriting practice
Bible
Magazines or newspapers with
propaganda examples
Art supplies to illustrate a time line

Additional Learning Activities

Section I

1. Discuss these questions about language:
    a. Who created language?
    b. What was Lucifer's plot?
    c. How do people abuse language?
    d. How did Adam use his gift of language?
2. List the following heteronyms on a chalk board or chart. Discuss the similar spellings, and different meanings and pronunciations.
    bass̄ (bas)   bass̄ (bas)
    dove (duv)   dove (dov)
3. With a friend or friends, make a mural showing Lucifer's plot, God's Creation of the world and Adam and Eve, and Adam's use of language. Use the Bible (Genesis 1 and 2) and the reading in Section I.
4. In a few paragraphs, tell in your own words how language began. Be sure your sentences are complete.

Section II

1. Discuss these questions about "Abused Language in the Garden."
    a. Why did God cast Lucifer out of heaven?
    b. How did Satan abuse language in the Garden of Eden?
    c. What happened to Adam and Eve when they ate the forbidden fruit?
2. Discuss "Cause and Effect." Use the following examples. Ask the students to supply a reasonable cause or effect for each item.
    a. a dying plant
    b. a rain storm
    c. broken glass
    d. an empty house
3. Present samples of propaganda to the class. Discuss the different techniques used to sell the product. Decide if facts or opinion are used. Is the advertising truthful? How do you decide?
4. Continue your mural. Add Satan in the garden, Adam and Eve eating the forbidden fruit, Adam and Eve leaving the garden, and Cain and Abel.

5. With a friend, create your own product. Illustrate your product showing each propaganda technique listed in Section II.
6. With two groups of students, play a game. Each team thinks of a root word. Taking turns, each team asks the other to add a prefix or suffix to the root word making a new word. Give one point for each correct new word. Subtract one point for each incorrect word.
7. Write a short story showing cause and effect.
8. Read a short story and write a summary of what you read.

Section III
1. Read selections from various types of books and articles. Discuss the author's purpose in each.
2. Discuss these questions about language:
   a. Why were the Shinar people building the Tower of Babel?
   b. Why did God confuse their language?
   c. How did the English language originate?
3. Complete your mural. Add Noah and the Flood and the Tower of Babel.
4. With a friend or friends, make a bulletin board illustrating idioms. Think of a "catchy" title. See Section III for ideas.
5. Make a time line about the history of language or the history of the English language. Be general.

Materials Needed for LIFEPAC

Required:

Suggested:
Note cards for taking notes
and organizing report information

Additional Learning Activities

Section I

1. Read paragraphs from magazines or newspapers to the students. Discuss the main idea of each paragraph. Discuss the details that support the main ideas.
2. Role play with a friend. Pretend your friend is new at your school. Converse with your friend only in commands and demands. Switch roles and have your friend converse with you courteously using polite requests.
3. With a friend, survey other students. Ask them what they know about a certain subject such as "whales." List the answers as fact or opinion. Report the results of the survey.
4. Write a thank-you note to a special friend or a person who has meant a lot to you in your Christian walk. Use each of the four kinds of sentences at least once. Remember Proverbs 25:11.
5. In one paragraph, write your opinion about your favorite Bible story.

Section II

1. List the following sentences on a chalkboard. Ask the students to identify the subject and predicate of each sentence.
   a. The invention of the telephone brought about world-wide changes.
   b. Voyager I gathered new data from Jupiter.
   c. Within the pages of an old book, he found a tattered note.
   d. The primitive tribe resisted any newcomers and their ways.
2. List the following sentences on a chalkboard. Ask students to supply adjectives and adverbs to the basic sentences. Discuss how the sentences change as different adjectives and adverbs are used.
   a. The plant grew.
   b. The Christians suffered persecution.
   c. The volunteer gave his time.
   d. The fox ran into a den.
3. Read Daniel, Chapter 3, in the Bible with a friend. Place the general events of the story in the order they happened. Illustrate each event.
4. Describe your favorite story character. Compare and contrast your favorite with a friend's favorite story character.
5. Read the book of Esther in the Bible. Write the character traits you admire in Esther.
6. Create word pictures by using figurative language. Write at least two metaphors and two similes.
7. Write a short paragraph telling how a cook may use adjectives. To help you, read a recipe for baking a cake.

Section III

1. Discuss topics for reports. Solicit ideas from the students. Distinguish between specific topics and those that are too broad. Discuss possible sources of information for each topic.
2. Demonstrate how to use resource books such as encyclopedias.
3. As a group, visit your school or city library. Locate reference books useful for report writing.
4. Discuss how to take good notes and how to use them to outline.
5. With a group of students, brainstorm possible ideas for report topics.
6. With a group of two or three other students, choose a topic. Each student should take one area of the topic to research. Combine your notes into outline form. Report your findings.
7. Choose a Bible topic. Take notes, outline, and write a written report.
8. Interview a missionary or pastor. Find out how and why he or she became a pastor or missionary. Give an oral report of your findings to the class.

Materials Needed for LIFEPAC

Required:

Suggested:
Construction paper or large manila
envelope
Magazines or newspapers to start
a file of sources for seed ideas

Additional Learning Activities

Section I

1. Discuss these questions about the legends:
   a. What is a legend?
   b. How do legends begin?
   c. How are legends passed on today?
2. Discuss the new words used in the story, "Arthur and the Sword in the Stone." Which words give a sense of long ago?
3. Discuss what makes a story a pleasure to read. Help the students to realize that the three basic elements for a good story are the kinds of words used, the action of the story, and the suspense. Let the students give examples of each from their favorite stories.
4. With a friend, read Daniel, Chapter 6, in the Bible. Make a list of the characteristics you admire in Daniel's life.
5. With several students, act out the story, "Arthur and the Sword in the Stone."
6. Read a library book. Write a short summary. Share it with the class.
7. Read another legend about King Arthur or Robin Hood. Judge its literary value by asking yourself the six questions in this section under judging a story as literature.

Section II

1. Demonstrate a dialogue. Converse with one student in front of the class. After the dialogue, ask the following questions:
   a. What is a "dialogue"?
   b. How many people do you need to have a dialogue?
2. Read the following sentences. Ask what is wrong with each sentence.
   a. He doesn't want any pie, *anyways*.
   b. I *except* your invitation.
   c. The girl played the piano *good*.
   d. My sister *learned* me to sew.
3. With a friend, write a dialogue. Choose two characters, such as a pioneer father and son on a wagon train, a bully to a small boy, a missionary to a primitive tribesman, and so forth. Be sure to use the language each would use in an actual dialogue. Read the dialogue to the class.
4. Play a game. With two teams, have each team write five sentences with poor word order. Exchange the sentences. The team to correctly rearrange the sentences first is the winner.

5. Write directions to a craft project in the correct sequence. See if a friend can figure out how to do the craft from your directions.
6. Create a cartoon strip with two main characters. Write a dialogue and illustrate the action.
7. Write a dialogue. Pretend you lived at the time when Jesus lived on earth. What would you say to Him? What might He say to you? Be sure to punctuate your dialogue correctly.

Section III

1. Display some interesting pictures from magazines or newspapers. Talk about seed ideas for writing stories. Ask students to respond to the pictures as sources of seed ideas. List the seed ideas on a chalkboard.
2. Develop one seed idea with the class. Outline a basic plot with a setting, characters, and action on a chalkboard.
3. With several friends, make a bulletin board about seed ides for writing stories. Use magazine or newspaper pictures and articles. See page 43 in this LIFEPAC for ideas.
4. Write five sentences. Have a friend correct them for spelling, punctuation, and word order. Discuss ways to improve your sentences.
5. Collect more sources of seed ideas for your folder or envelope. See page 44 in this LIFEPAC. Make a list of possible story ideas and characters.
6. Use one of your seed ideas and write a short story. Place it in a folder. Illustrate your story where possible.

Materials Needed for LIFEPAC

Required: Suggested:
                                   Dictionary

Additional Learning Activities

Section I

1. Discuss story poems. Ask these questions:
   a. Why do you think storytellers used poetry to tell a story?
   b. What were story poems that were sung called?
   c. What do poets write in rather than paragraphs?
2. Read "Landing of the Pilgrim Fathers in New England." Ask the students to locate some of the poetic expressions. Discuss what they mean. Ask the students to find descriptive words. Ask how the poetic language helps them to see the picture more clearly.
3. Discuss the story poem, "Barbara Frietche." Was the gallant behavior of General Stonewall Jackson a symbol of respect for one's enemy, respect for women, or respect for old age?
4. Read a favorite poem or one from this LIFEPAC to the class. Discuss the rhythm and its musical quality. Write a line or two from the poem on a chalkboard. Discuss how the rhythm is found in the beat or stress. Underline the stressed syllables. Have the students tap out the rhythm.
5. With a group of students, choral read the story poem, "Landing of the Pilgrim Fathers in New England." Practice each stanza carefully in order to carry the intensity of the poem to the end. Perform the choral reading for other students.
6. With a friend, illustrate stanzas one and two from "Landing of the Pilgrim Fathers in New England." Try to capture the feeling of the poem in your drawing.
7. Memorize a favorite poem. Recite it to the other students.

Section II

1. Discuss these questions about ballads:
   a. How many lines are usually in each stanza of a ballad?
   b. What story is told in the ballad, "King John and the Abbot of Canterbury"?
2. Discuss palindromes, conundrums, puns, and limericks. Write an example of each on the chalkboard. Discuss the form of each and how they "play on words." Ask the students to make up other examples. Write a few on the chalkboard.
3. With several students, act out the ballad, "King John and the Abbot of Canterbury."
4. With a friend, write several conundrums. Illustrate each one. Place your conundrums and illustrations on the bulletin board.

5. Read another ballad, such as one from the Robin Hood stories. Write the main idea of the ballad in your own words.

6. Write a limerick about an animal. Begin your limerick "There once was a(n) (animal) named (name)." Add the limerick to your poetry booklet.

Section III

1. Discuss what makes a poem inspirational. Discuss the inspirational qualities in the poem, "The Village Blacksmith."

2. Write an example of each of the following items on a chalkboard or chart: metaphor, simile, and personification. Discuss each example. Solicit examples from the students. List them on the chalkboard or chart.

3. Write a rhymed quatrain with a friend. You supply the first line. Your friend will write the second line, and so on. Share the poem with the class.

4. With a group of students, choose a free verse passage from the Bible. Prepare a choral reading to be presented to your class.

5. Write a poem using at least two poetic devices such as metaphor, simile, or personification.

6. Write an inspirational poem. Look through some verses of songs in a hymnal for ideas.

Materials Needed for LIFEPAC

Required: Suggested:
                                             Dictionary

Additional Learning Activities

Section I

1. Discuss the following causes and effects. Ask the students to complete each one orally. Each one may be a cause or an effect depending on how it is completed.
    a. The milk spilled on the floor -
    b. The bird fell from the nest -
    c. The forest fire blazed all night -
    d. The river froze over completely -
2. Discuss the following questions and items about personal reactions.
    a. How would you react to finding a mouse in a drawer? Would we all react the same way?
    b. How would you react to the following situations? A lost pet; a visit from a friend; dropping a lunch tray in the cafeteria.
    c. List some reaction words on a chalkboard.
3. Create a play about "A Voyage to Lilliput." Perform it for the class.
4. With a friend, make a bulletin board showing causes and effects.
5. Write a personal reaction to one of the following ideas or choose your own idea. Remember to use reaction words.
    a. A bear awakens you at your campsite.
    b. You receive the best grade in class on an important test.
    c. Your best friend breaks his arm right before the last game of the season.

Section II

1. Write a common noun and a proper noun on a chalkboard. Discuss the differences between the two. Ask for more examples of each.
2. Discuss possessive nouns. Review the three rules on page 32 of this LIFEPAC. List the following words on a chalkboard. Ask several students to come to the board and write the possessive form of each one.
    a. toy
    b. ladies
    c. trees
    d. oxen
    e. painter
    f. ship
3. Write the following sentences on a chalkboard. Ask the students to identify the nouns used as subjects and the nouns used as objects of the verbs.
    a. The monkey ate a banana.
    b. The pitcher threw a ball.
    c. The early settlers hunted the buffalo.
    d. The new couple hired a painter to do the job.

4. Write a paragraph or two without using any pronouns. Ask a friend to replace as many nouns as he can with pronouns.
5. Write a tongue twister using some of your spelling words with an /sh/sound. See the example in Section II of this LIFEPAC. See if a friend can say your tongue twister fast.
6. Write Psalm 23. Replace each pronoun with a noun or possessive noun. Example: He (the Lord) maketh me (your name) to lie down in green pastures.
7. Write a story using ten proper nouns.

Section III

1. Discuss these questions about Christian judgment.
   a. As a Christian, how do we decide what is right or wrong?
   b. Read John 14:6. What does this verse mean?
   c. What is Christian judgment? Explain that Christian judgment is when we judge whether an action, what we read, or what we see is right or wrong according to Christian principles.
2. Read the following pairs of events. Ask the students to infer what happened between each of the events.
   a. (1) Jeff went horseback riding for the first time and the horse he chose was not exactly gentle.
      (2) Suddenly, Jeff found himself face down in the dirt.
   b. (1) The Smith family built a new home by the edge of a river, much to the dismay of the local residents.
      (2) After the first spring rains, the Smiths had to evacuate their new home.
3. With a friend, read some factual information on a subject of your choice. Write five facts about the subject. Together, write five personal opinions you may have on the subject.
4. Write a paragraph expressing a particular mood. See if a friend can identify the mood.
5. Read an article from a newspaper or magazine. Write the main idea.
6. Read Luke 8:22 through 25 in the Bible. Write the main idea and mood of the passage.

Section IV

1. Discuss adjectives. Ask the students to give you examples of adjectives that tell what kind, how many, and which one. Write the examples on a chalkboard.
2. Write the following basic sentence on a chalkboard. *The cat chased a mouse.* Ask the students to expand the sentence with adjectives. See how many different adjectives can be used. Discuss the position of adjectives in a sentence.

3. Make a bulletin board with a friend. Write and illustrate five basic sentences. Then, write and illustrate the same sentences after you have expanded them with adjectives. Example: <u>The cow jumped over the moon.</u> AND <u>The large, black and white cow jumped over a full moon.</u> Try to show the contrast between the sentences with your drawings.

4. Play a game with two groups of students. Each team writes three sentences with adjectives. Each team scrambles each of the three sentences. The teams exchange the sentences. The first team to correctly unscramble the sentences wins.

5. Describe your bedroom using as many adjectives as you can.

6. Write a silly story. Begin the story by expanding the following basic sentence: *A giant met a dragon.* See the examples in Section IV of this LIFEPAC.

Materials Needed for LIFEPAC

Required:

Suggested:

Yolen, Jane, illustrated by K. Barbour
<u>A Sip of Aesop</u>, 1995.

Barnes-Murphy, Frances and Rowan
<u>The Fables of Aesop</u>, 1994

or any book containing Aesop's Fables

Additional Learning Activities

Section I

1. Discuss verbs of action and verbs of being. Have the students give examples of each. Make a list on the chalkboard. Change any singular verbs to plural and any plural verbs to singular.
2. Make a chart with the following headings: past tense, present tense, future tense, present perfect, past perfect, and future perfect. Write one example under each heading. Ask the students to think of more examples. Write them on the chart. Use the examples in sentences and discuss how the tense shows time.
3. Discuss regular and irregular verbs. Make a list of each. See if the students can discover why irregular verbs are irregular.
4. Demonstrate how a verb is changed to a present participle by adding *-ing*, and a past participle by adding *-ed*, *-d*, *-t*, *-en*, or *-n*. Ask the students if they can use a participle as a verb alone. Demonstrate how a participle becomes an adjective modifier.
5. Make a bulletin board with a friend or friends. Illustrate verb tenses. Title the bulletin board, "A Tense in Time." Use several different basic sentences. Write and illustrate each basic sentence in the present tense, past tense, and future tense. Examples:
    a. "Joe, drop the jar."
    b. Joe dropped the jar.
    c. Joe will drop the jar.
6. With a friend, make a list of participles that may be used as modifiers with a word each may modify. Example: *sleeping* boy.
7. Write a letter to a friend. Use at least five contractions.
8. Write a paragraph using the present, past, and future verb tenses at least twice.
9. Read about Moses in Exodus, Chapter 3, in the Bible. Memorize verses 13 and 14.

Section II

1. Read one of Aesop's fables to the class. Ask these questions:
    a. Who are the characters?
    b. What happened in the fable?
    c. What is the fable trying to teach us or what is the moral?
2. Read Luke 10:30 through 37 (The Good Samaritan) to the class. Discuss these questions:
    a. Why do you think Jesus told parables?
    b. Who are the characters in this parable?
    c. What happened in this parable?
    d. What spiritual truth was Jesus teaching through the parable?
3. With several students, make a mural that illustrates one of Aesop's fables.
4. Write a fable. Remember the characteristics of a fable. Be sure your fable has the literary elements of a good story.
5. Choose one topic and write a parable. Outline the parable by using the elements of a good story listed in Section II of this LIFEPAC.

Section III

1. Discuss adverbs. Ask the students to give examples of adverbs for the following headings on a chalkboard: how, when, and where. Ask the students what the purpose of an adverb is.
2. Write the following sentence on a chalkboard. "He was an extremely active athlete." Underline the word *extremely*. Ask the students what word it modifies. Explain that *extremely* is an adverb modifying the adjective, *active*. Show how it does not modify *athlete* by reading the word pairs, *extremely athlete* and *extremely active*. Discuss how *extremely athlete* does not make sense.
3. Demonstrate how to make adverbs from adjectives by adding the *-ly* suffix. Use the following examples:

Adjectives	Adverbs
a. a <u>sad</u> boy	cried <u>sadly</u>
b. a <u>gentle</u> breeze	blew <u>gently</u>
c. a <u>beautiful</u> day	sparkled <u>beautifully</u>
d. a <u>quiet</u> person	a <u>quietly</u> kind person

4. With a friend, expand several basic sentences with different adverbs. Illustrate the sentence pairs to show how different adverbs change the meaning of the basic sentence. Examples:
    a. The lion ran *quickly*.
    b. The lion ran *slowly*.
5. In a paragraph, compare two or three objects. Use adverbs showing comparison.
6. Write a paragraph using adverbs that modify verbs, adjectives, and adverbs.

Materials Needed for LIFEPAC

Required:

Suggested:
Bible
encyclopedia and other
reference books

Additional Learning Activities

Section I

1. Discuss these questions with your class:
   a. Discuss fluency skills. Ask the students if they always read at the same speed. Do they always read fast? Do they always read slow? Explain the differences between scanning, skimming, and reading slowly for details. Demonstrate each skill.
   b. Provide the same reading material for a group of students. Ask the students to scan the material for general content. Limit the amount of time. Then ask the students to skim the material for specific information you have previously chosen. Set a time limit. Finally, ask the students to read slowly for details.
2. With a friend, scan the same article. Time yourselves. See who can find the correct general content of the article first, in the least amount of time. Try the same thing with several more articles.
3. Read an article. Choose some specific information from the article. Ask a friend to skim the article to find the information. Time your friend.
4. Read John 10:1 through 18 in the Bible. Before you read, pray that God will teach you something from His Word. First scan the passage for its general content. Write what you think it is. Skim the passage for certain details. Write several down. Finally, read the passage slowly. Write down as many details as you can remember.
5. Choose several articles to scan and skim. Time yourself. See if you can improve your time and yet scan and skim effectively.

Section II

1. Display several graphic aids for the students such as maps, illustrations, charts, and diagrams. Discuss what information can be gained from each one. Ask why graphic aids are helpful.
2. Choose a short article to read to the students. Ask the students to help you outline the article on a chalkboard. Emphasize topics, subtopics, correct sequence, and using capitals correctly.
3. With a friend, create a bulletin board about graphic aids. Locate or make an example of several different kinds of graphic aids.
4. Choose at least two kinds of graphic aids and find an example of each one. With a friend, list the information you can learn from each one.
5. Read a short story, article, or Bible story. Illustrate an exciting part of the story. Write a caption for your illustration.
6. Outline a favorite story, article, or Bible story.
7. Make a diagram of a favorite art project. Example: How to build a bird house.
8. Make a map of your neighborhood, city, or state. Identify important places.

Section III

1. Display several examples of literature (short story, novel, biography, history, poetry, articles, etc.). Discuss the differences in each one.
2. Place some objects before the students (flower, rock, book, etc.). Ask the students to state some facts about each one, and then some opinions about each one.
3. Discuss fiction and nonfiction. Ask the students to give examples of each one.
4. With a group of students, find a good play or create one of your own. Present the play for the class.
5. With a group of students, choral read Psalms 95:1 through 7a.
6. Memorize a poem.
7. Read a novel or biography. Write a book report or summary of the book.
8. Write five facts and five opinions about a subject from an encyclopedia.

Materials Needed for LIFEPAC

Required:

Suggested:
12" x 18" piece of construction paper
paper fasteners or yarn
writing paper
(optional) poster paints and potato half

Additional Learning Activities

Section I

1. Discuss these questions:
    a. What are some questions you can ask yourself about the value of a story as literature?
    b. How do you judge the characters in a story?
    c. What three elements make a story a pleasure to read?
    d. What are some types of fiction? Nonfiction?
    e. How is rhythm made in poetry?
    f. What are some of the poetic devices used in poetry?
    g. What is an inspirational poem?
    h. What is the difference between a common noun and a proper noun?
    i. What are three characteristics of a short story?
2. With several students, make a bulletin board displaying many of the types of literature.
3. Write a class poetry booklet for your parents. Each student contributes one or two poems.
4. Locate a novel, short story, or legend in the library. Read one and write a summary of the book. Judge its literary value by the six questions in this LIFEPAC. Decide if the book contained the three elements that make a story a pleasure to read.

Section II

1. Discuss these questions:
    a. What may an author's purpose be?
    b. What does "finding the main idea" mean?
    c. What is cause and effect?
    d. How do we make Christian judgments?
    e. What are verb tenses? Name them and give examples of each one.
    f. What is a participle? How is it used in a sentence?
    g. How do you change an adjective into an adverb?
2. Choose an article. Write comprehension questions about the article. Have a friend read the same article. See if he can answer your questions correctly.
3. With a group of students read several articles in a newspaper or magazine. Together make Christian judgments about what you read.
4. Illustrate the literal meaning of several idioms.
5. Write two or three cause and effect relationships. Identify each one.

Section III

1. Discuss these questions:
    a. Should you always read fast?
    b. When should you read slow?
    c. What are two rapid reading skills?
    d. What are some kinds of graphic aids?
    e. What information can you gain from each kind of graphic aid?
    f. Why is outlining important?
    g. What should you include in a summary?
    h. How would you compare and contrast David and Goliath?
    i. What do you do when you compare and contrast?
    j. How can we use reading skills to study the Bible?
    k. What are the four kinds of sentences and how do you punctuate each one?
    l. What is a dialogue? Give an example.
    m. What is a personal reaction? Give an example.
2. With a friend make a time line of a portion of American or Biblical history. Examples:
    a. Landing of the Pilgrims up to the Civil War
    b. Adam to David
3. With a friend, each of you write five sentences. Exchange the sentences and improve them by adding both adjectives and adverbs.
4. With a friend, write a dialogue. The dialogue should be a conversation in which one friend is explaining to the other how to know Jesus Christ as personal Saviour.
5. Make a map of a Biblical time. Examples:
    a. Paul's missionary journeys.
    b. Palestine at the time of Christ.
6. Read Psalm 1:1 through 3. Study the passage by charting the information.

Notes

LIFEPAC TEST

1. college   The local <u>college</u> invited all the grade school students to visit the campus.   college
2. expense   Colleen's family decided to vacation at home because of the <u>expense</u> of travel.   expense
3. roaster   The <u>roaster</u> will not fit in the oven when th door is closed.   roaster
4. mountain   The snow on the <u>mountain</u> was whiter than the clouds.   mountain
5. freedom   Our country's <u>freedom</u> is very precious to us.   freedom
6. arrange   To <u>arrange</u> the furniture properly, the mover checked the floor plan.   arrange
7. toothache   Nobody enjoys a <u>toothache.</u>   toothache
8. boycott   Many shoppers decided to <u>boycott</u> the store because of the poor customer service.   boycott
9. fewer   Children bought <u>fewer</u> candy bars this year than last year.   fewer
10. Tuesday   After next <u>Tuesday,</u> most of the children will know if they can go on the hike.   Tuesday
11. peaceful   Our visitors enjoyed the <u>peaceful</u> Sunday worshiping God.   peaceful
12. railway   The <u>railway</u> station was crowded with weekend travelers.   railway
13. vowel   Language students soon discover that the <u>vowel</u> is silent in many words.   vowel
14. abound   Fish <u>abound</u> in that creek, so we caught plenty of them.   abound
15. saucer   A cup and <u>saucer</u> go together like salt and pepper.   saucer
16. elate   The captain tried to <u>elate</u> his team members, even though defeat seemed certain.   elate
17. proudly   He <u>proudly</u> showed his new bicycle to his friends because he had earned it himself.   proudly
18. creature   You are a <u>creature</u> made by God and loved by Him.   creature
19. homestead   We visited the old <u>homestead</u>, where my father grew up.   homestead
20. boiling   <u>Boiling</u> water is one way of purifying it.   boiling
21. prowler   The nighttime <u>prowler</u> turned out to be a stray cat.   prowler
22. climate   A warm <u>climate</u> in the southwest attracts many winter visitors.   climate
23. achieve   You can <u>achieve</u> mighty things through Christ.   achieve

LIFEPAC TEST cont...

24.	mistake	According to the judge, it was a mistake anyone could have made.	mistake
25.	active	Many grandparents remain active in their old age.	active
26.	booklet	If the booklet of instructions had been available, the youngster could have put his own toy together.	booklet
27.	sower	The sower went forth to sow seeds.	sower
28.	advise	Everybody wanted to advise the boy's friend what to do, but he would not listen.	advise
29.	sweeten	To sweeten the icing for the cake, the baker used honey.	sweeten
30.	doily	A fancy doily was on the plate under the dish.	doily
31.	eastern	Just before dawn, the eastern sky begins to lighten.	eastern
32.	figure	To play the game, we had to guess what figure was missing from each picture.	figure
33.	believe	Believe on the Lord Jesus Christ and you will be saved.	believe
34.	royal	One of the prettiest of all colors is royal blue.	royal
35.	tower	From the top of the tower, you could see across the entire valley.	tower
36.	smoothly	The voyage started out smoothly but ended in a storm.	smoothly
37.	flounder	Loss of steering control caused the boat to flounder in the waves.	flounder
38.	caution	The road signs were there to caution motorists about a danger down the road.	caution
39.	secure	They all felt secure inside the shelter.	secure
40.	praying	The teacher announced that praying would be the first thing done in her class everyday.	praying

ALTERNATE LIFEPAC TEST

1. account   The boy's savings <u>account</u> at the bank was   account
                 growing every month.
2. forehead   With his hand on his <u>forehead,</u> he appeared   forehead
                 to be thinking deeply.
3. smoothly   Cars rode <u>smoothly</u> on the new highway through   smoothly
                 town.
4. eschew   He tried to <u>eschew</u> wrongdoing by choosing good eschew
                 companions.
5. creature   Man, the <u>creature</u>, should worship God, the   creature
                 creator.
6. boiling   The young child was warned to stay away from   boiling
                 the <u>boiling</u> water.
7. coward   A <u>coward</u> will usually back down if someone   coward
                 stands up to him.
8. freedom   The price of <u>freedom</u> is remembered every   freedom
                 Memorial Day.
9. poison   Everyone was aware that a bottle containing   poison
                 <u>poison</u> should be plainly marked.
10. advise   All parents should <u>advise</u> their children to   advise
                 accept Jesus as Saviour.
11. roaster   After the chicken was placed in the <u>roaster,</u>   roaster
                 it was roasted for two hours.
12. pointing   The compass needle is always <u>pointing</u> toward   pointing
                 true north.
13. sweeten   Sugar was on the table in the event some of the sweeten
                 people wanted to <u>sweeten</u> their breakfast cereal.
14. secure   The night watchman's job was to <u>secure</u> the locks secure
                 on all the doors.
15. minute   God is concerned about the <u>minute</u> details of   minute
                 your life.
16. eastern   The weatherman expected the <u>eastern</u> half of   eastern
                 the nation to have fair weather.
17. saucer   She was somewhat embarrassed when the <u>saucer</u>   saucer
                 fell on the floor.
18. obscure   He was an <u>obscure</u> clerk in an office before his obscure
                 invention made him famous.
19. tower   Overlooking the city was a <u>tower</u> built out of   tower
                 huge blocks of stone.
20. booklet   The <u>booklet</u> provided all the answers to John's booklet
                 questions.
21. loader   Several men watched as the huge <u>loader</u> cleared loader
                 rubble from the demolished building.

ALTERNATE LIFEPAC TEST cont...

22.	royal	The royal family received worldwide acclaim on coronation day.	royal
23.	powder	Keeping their powder dry was a necessity for soldiers in the American Revolution.	powder
24.	railway	The old railway depot was turned into a museum.	railway
25.	joyous	There is joyous singing in heaven whenever a person receives Jesus Christ as Saviour.	joyous
26.	achieve	To achieve anything worthwhile requires continued dedication to the task at hand.	achieve
27.	failure	A failure at the power company caused all the electricity to be off for two hours.	failure
28.	prowler	When the prowler showed up, the police were waiting to seize him.	prowler
29.	voyage	The young lad looked forward to the long voyage across the ocean.	voyage
30.	caution	Yellow traffic signs usually mean caution for the motorist entering the area.	caution
31.	treasure	The Bible clearly teaches that your treasure is in heaven where it will last forever.	treasure
32.	climate	The climate seemed to be changing, according to weather bureau information.	climate
33.	wayward	Often during floods, rivers will follow a wayward path.	wayward
34.	proudly	The rooster marched proudly around the barnyard when visitors were there.	proudly
35.	jointly	It was an agreement made jointly by the two brothers.	jointly
36.	growing	The Bible says we all should be growing in grace.	growing
37.	crooked	Except for a slightly crooked leg, the animal appeared to be perfect.	crooked
38.	suppose	It is better to get all the facts than to suppose the events took place.	suppose
39.	mountain	Faith that could move a mountain is mentioned by Jesus in the Bible.	mountain
40.	decoy	A decoy is sometimes used to attract wild ducks to where hunters are on a lake.	decoy

LIFEPAC TEST

1.	minute	The clock showed just one <u>minute</u> before midnight.	minute
2.	landscape	White, billowy clouds could be seen above the <u>landscape</u>.	landscape
3.	childhood	The old man fondly recalled memories of his <u>childhood</u> days.	childhood
4.	laid	After the crucifixion, Jesus' friends <u>laid</u> his body in a borrowed tomb.	laid
5.	afternoon	By the middle of the <u>afternoon</u>, ocean breezes had blown away the fog.	afternoon
6.	doctor	The <u>doctor</u> knew exactly what to do for Tom's broken leg.	doctor
7.	grapefruit	Mother always served <u>grapefruit</u> for breakfast.	grapefruit
8.	business	"I must be about my Father's <u>business</u>" is a famous statement by Jesus.	business
9.	inlet	The ship's navigator searched for the <u>inlet</u> leading to the inland port.	inlet
10.	keyboard	The piano teacher suggested more practice on the <u>keyboard</u>.	keyboard
11.	separate	The school board decided that the gymnasium and auditorium should be <u>separate</u> buildings.	separate
12.	deerskin	The Old West mountain men wore <u>deerskin</u> coats.	deerskin
13.	raise	A tear rolled down the soldier's cheek whenever he saw a flag <u>raise</u>.	raise
14.	evildoer	The Bible warns the <u>evildoer</u> many times.	evildoer
15.	among	An unpopular tax collector was <u>among</u> Jesus' disciples.	among
16.	fisherman	The <u>fisherman</u> checked his nets everyday.	fisherman
17.	hardship	Pioneers had to endure <u>hardship</u> during the early days of our nation.	hardship
18.	believe	Part of Romans 10:9 says, "If thou shalt <u>believe</u> in thine heart that God hath raised Him from the dead, thou shalt be saved."	believe
19.	moonlight	By the <u>moonlight,</u> the patrol could see which route to follow.	moonlight
20.	forty	Jesus spent <u>forty</u> days in the wilderness without food.	forty

Now we will complete the test with a series of word contractions. Remember to write the apostrophe in the correct place within the word. The first contraction is:

21.	should've	Everyone thought the boys <u>should've</u> done better in the tug of war game.	should've

LIFEPAC TEST cont...

22.	we'll	If we'll just trust the Lord more, we can begin to see some great things happen.	we'll
23.	he's	They say he's the one who will win the contest.	he's
24.	would've	It would've been helpful if the team had practiced longer.	would've
25.	it's	My mother said it's too cold to go outside without a coat on.	it's
26.	you've	According to the travel folder, you've not seen Germany unless you've seen the Rhine River.	you've
27.	let's	We could hear the group singing, "Let's just praise the Lord.	let's
28.	could've	If rain had not stopped the game, the score could've been higher.	could've
29.	shouldn't	The youngster was told that he shouldn't go beyond the bridge.	shouldn't
30.	don't	Do you wonder why some trees don't lose their leaves in the winter?	don't
31.	we've	My family feels that we've got a lot to thank God for.	we've
32.	shan't	It was the first time many in the audience heard the word "shan't" used in place of "shall not".	shan't
33.	I've	The lad exclaimed, "I've thought about that for a long time."	I've
34.	they'd	While working in the fields, they'd often think of the relaxing time coming at the end of the day.	they'd
35.	wouldn't	Advice from his friends wouldn't have changed his mind.	wouldn't
36.	she'll	They say she'll be much better after the recovery period.	she'll
37.	isn't	That isn't necessarily what is expected of the farmer.	isn't
38.	we'd	Without hope in Christ, we'd all be miserable people.	we'd
39.	you're	Tim said, "You're right, Sally, the next test is tomorrow.	you're
40.	haven't	The store clerks haven't the slightest idea where a grandfather clock can be repaired.	haven't

ALTERNATE LIFEPAC TEST

1.	jaybird	All that chattering came from a single jaybird sitting on the fence.	jaybird
2.	minute	The particles of metal were so minute they required a microscope to be seen.	minute
3.	moonlight	Swift-moving clouds occasionally prevented the moonlight from shining in the window.	moonlight
4.	busy	The intersection was busy all day on Saturday.	busy
5.	separate	On his uncle's farm, Jim learned to separate the milk from the cream.	separate
6.	brand-new	What a thrill it was to wear a brand-new suit.	brand-new
7.	keyboard	The piano tuner reworked the keyboard at the upper end.	keyboard
8.	inlet	An inlet to the water pump was clogged up.	inlet
9.	among	She was happy to be numbered among the Christians.	among
10.	landscape	Every landscape changes appearance at different times during the day.	landscape
11.	believe	To believe on Christ means to place your faith in Him for your salvation.	believe
12.	hardship	Holding two jobs worked a hardship on the young man.	hardship
13.	forty	After forty miles on the road, the old truck began to act up.	forty
14.	business	Following the holiday, it was "business as usual" in the downtown area.	business
15.	childhood	Common childhood diseases include chicken pox and measles.	childhood
16.	raise	God said He would raise up a people who would worship Him.	raise
17.	afternoon	Just before the afternoon classes, the principal gave a brief talk.	afternoon
18.	doctor	The doctor had cared for the family for over thirty years.	doctor
19.	grapefruit	Janet lived next to a large orchard where grapefruit and orange trees grew.	grapefruit
20.	deerskin	Two hundred years ago, deerskin coats were quite common wearing apparel.	deerskin

The rest of the spelling test consists of spelling contractions. Remember to write the apostrophe in the correct place within the word, starting with:

21.	they're	Whenever they're lagging behind, the mother duck swims back around her ducklings.	they're

ALTERNATE LIFEPAC TEST cont...

22.	you've	Now that <u>you've</u> been to the state park, maybe you would tell us how to get there.	you've
23.	don't	The youngsters must decide whether they do or they <u>don't</u> want to camp out all night.	don't
24.	he's	When <u>he's</u> not very tired, the dog will bark all night.	he's
25.	can't	Lucy said she <u>can't</u> wait until her next birthday so she can have a party.	can't
26.	we'd	The other teacher said <u>we'd</u> be able to go with her class some other time.	we'd
27.	let's	Without grumbling, <u>let's</u> see if we can move all the furniture into the house.	let's
28.	I've	The ten year-old boy said, "<u>I've</u> decided to follow Jesus."	I've
29.	won't	As strong as it is, the bulldozer <u>won't</u> be able to move the huge boulder.	won't
30.	you're	The guide had said <u>you're</u> on the right road if you pass a large weeping willow tree.	you're
31.	haven't	Many young people in other countries <u>haven't</u> had much opportunity to learn about Jesus.	haven't
32.	we'll	With David on our team, <u>we'll</u> be hard to beat.	we'll
33.	she's	Betty told the teacher <u>she's</u> not sure about her answers to the last three questions.	she's
34.	isn't	Flying a kite near telephone lines <u>isn't</u> a wise thing to do.	isn't
35.	they'd	The park ranger said <u>they'd</u> be better off not to follow the upper trail.	they'd
36.	it's	Now that <u>it's</u> noon, we ought to stop for lunch.	it's
37.	she'll	When the old sailboat comes back to port, <u>she'll</u> have to be repaired.	she'll
38.	could've	Many <u>could've</u> been saved if they had put their trust in Jesus.	could've
39.	shouldn't	Nevertheless, the postman said they <u>shouldn't</u> expect the letter to arrive until next week.	shouldn't
40.	wouldn't	<u>Wouldn't</u> it be great if everyone on earth decided to follow Christ?	wouldn't

LIFEPAC TEST

1.	chalk	Writing with <u>chalk</u> caused a screeching noise.	chalk
2.	wrist	Father's <u>wrist</u> watch always kept accurate time.	wrist
3.	formal	The teacher gave <u>formal</u> notice about doing the extra homework.	formal
4.	casual	We will be wise not to be <u>casual</u> about our commitment to Christ.	casual
5.	freight	The large truck carried <u>freight</u> weighing twenty tons.	freight
6.	salmon	One fishing boat loaded with <u>salmon</u> was lost in the storm.	salmon
7.	repel	Trying to <u>repel</u> the swarm of bees was difficult for the beekeeper.	repel
8.	folks	Several young people visited the old <u>folks</u> home.	folks
9.	knot	A <u>knot</u> in a wet rope is often hard to untie.	knot
10.	betrayal	The history class studied about the <u>betrayal</u> of a young soldier.	betrayal
11.	underneath	The Psalms mention that "<u>underneath</u> are the everlasting arms" of God.	underneath
12.	leadership	Good <u>leadership</u> from the quarterback helped the team to win.	leadership
13.	wrench	A misplaced <u>wrench</u> means the tool box is incomplete.	wrench
14.	advance	Kenny watched the clock <u>advance</u> one more minute.	advance
15.	gush	When the pipes thawed, the water began to <u>gush</u> from the open faucet.	gush
16.	newscaster	The local <u>newscaster</u> mentioned our school's scholastic record.	newscaster
17.	knowledge	<u>Knowledge</u> of God leads to wisdom.	knowledge
18.	flight	Watching the <u>flight</u> of birds captured their full attention.	flight
19.	joyous	Worship should be a <u>joyous</u> time for the Christian.	joyous
20.	trickle	Sugar began to <u>trickle</u> from the torn sack.	trickle
21.	admit	The man who had been arrested finally had to <u>admit</u> he was guilty.	admit
22.	kneel	Carl's trick horse was taught to <u>kneel</u> on a barrel.	kneel
23.	preserve	Action was taken to <u>preserve</u> wildlife in the state park.	preserve
24.	daughter	Uncle John's <u>daughter</u> is our cousin.	daughter
25.	maintenance	The highway <u>maintenance</u> yard is just outside of town.	maintenance

LIFEPAC TEST cont...

26.	woodpecker	A redheaded woodpecker was standing on the nearby telephone pole.	woodpecker
27.	glisten	On a clear day, the sun would glisten on the water.	glisten
28.	insult	Do not insult Tom by treating him like a baby.	insult
29.	destroy	Adding too much water to the soup will destroy its flavor.	destroy
30.	wrestle	The Bible tells that Jacob had to wrestle with an angel.	wrestle
31.	compliment	Giving someone a compliment is a good way to help them.	compliment
32.	attract	Several of his teammates tried to attract his attention.	attract
33.	seventeenth	Kevin expected to visit his uncle on the seventeenth day of the month.	seventeenth
34.	bristle	To prepare her pony for the parade, Sherri used a large bristle brush.	bristle
35.	fiction	A literary work whose contents are not based on fact is fiction.	fiction
36.	jewelry	Richard discovered that jewelry was too expensive a gift.	jewelry
37.	knight	The story was about a knight from King Arthur's court.	knight
38.	encourage	She tried to encourage her little brother to read his book.	encourage
39.	fasten	The campers had a difficult time trying to fasten the tent ropes during the storm.	fasten
40.	automatic	An automatic sprinkler system protected the building from fire.	automatic

ALTERNATE LIFEPAC TEST

1.	uneasy	Larry felt uneasy about leaving his bicycle in front of the store.	uneasy
2.	faithfully	Many people faithfully attend the nearby church.	faithfully
3.	hasten	Mother tried to hasten the preparation of our lunch.	hasten
4.	fact	The mayor repeated the fact that he was elected by a large vote.	fact
5.	sorrowful	Losing a pet can make a person sorrowful for a while.	sorrowful
6.	sigh	A sigh of relief was heard after the test.	sigh
7.	neighborhood	Everyone in the neighborhood heard the loud explosion.	neighborhood
8.	available	The store clerk said more paper would be available tomorrow.	available
9.	flight	Through binoculars, Freddy watched the flight of birds.	flight
10.	knowledge	The preacher said knowledge of our real nature is found in the Bible.	knowledge
11.	discourage	No one could discourage the people from building a church.	discourage
12.	wrench	The hardware store carried the right size wrench for the job.	wrench
13.	chalk	A chalk mark showed where the coat should be taken in.	chalk
14.	meaningful	The students found that the program was meaningful to their studies.	meaningful
15.	trickle	A small hole allowed the water to trickle out of the barrel.	trickle
16.	deny	Jesus foretold that Peter would deny Him three times.	deny
17.	advance	The soldiers were told to advance after midnight.	advance
18.	stalk	Grasshoppers started to eat a stalk of corn.	stalk
19.	freight	Trains carry mostly freight.	freight
20.	somersault	Turning a somersault was easy for Jack.	somersault
21.	leadership	The president showed leadership in running his company.	leadership
22.	exceedingly	Summer rains made the soil exceedingly wet.	exceedingly

ALTERNATE LIFEPAC TEST cont…

23.	wrist	A broken wrist usually has to be in a cast for several weeks.	wrist
24.	retreat	Tammy enjoyed the summer at her parents' retreat in the mountains.	retreat
25.	preserve	Psalm 121 says the Lord "shall preserve thy soul."	preserve
26.	wreckage	Searchers finally found the wreckage from the plane crash.	wreckage
27.	underneath	Interesting insects can be seen underneath rocks.	underneath
28.	remainder	Mother placed the remainder of the dinner food on a small table.	remainder
29.	woodpecker	You could hear the woodpecker a block away.	woodpecker
30.	casual	The teacher never displayed a casual attitude toward her students.	casual
31.	soothingly	The teacher spoke soothingly to the frightened child.	soothingly
32.	daughter	Neighbors kept their daughter home when she disobeyed.	daughter
33.	insult	Never insult another student by calling him stupid.	insult
34.	repel	A special oil was used to repel insects.	repel
35.	inauguration	The class read about the inauguration of the President.	inauguration
36.	newscaster	When reporting the accident, the voice of the newscaster was excited.	newscaster
37.	foolishness	Everyone laughed at the foolishness of the clowns.	foolishness
38.	glisten	Icicles glisten as soon as the sun shines on them.	glisten
39.	attract	In science, we saw how a magnet will attract metal.	attract
40.	joyous	Christmas is always a joyous holiday.	joyous

LIFEPAC TEST

1.	add	Can you <u>add</u> those numbers?	add
2.	banner	A large <u>banner</u> hangs at the front of our church.	banner
3.	castle	Have you ever visited a <u>castle</u>?	castle
4.	egg	I eat an <u>egg</u> every morning for breakfast.	egg
5.	filled	Every seat was <u>filled</u> in church last Sunday.	filled
6.	ghost	He tried to scare me by saying he had seen a <u>ghost</u>.	ghost
7.	gnat	I've been bitten by a <u>gnat</u>!	gnat
8.	listen	I like to <u>listen</u> to my grandfather's stories.	listen
9.	muscle	He pulled a <u>muscle</u> when he jumped.	muscle
10.	pneumonia	My friend is in the hospital with <u>pneumonia</u>.	pneumonia
11.	celebrate	Tomorrow, we <u>celebrate</u> my brother's birthday.	celebrate
12.	celestial	Stars are <u>celestial</u> bodies.	celestial
13.	compliment	Teachers often <u>compliment</u> their student's good work.	compliment
14.	confident	I am <u>confident</u> that my doctor is a good one.	confident
15.	cough	To <u>cough</u> during a concert is disturbing.	cough
16.	cucumber	This is a <u>cucumber</u> from my garden.	cucumber
17.	cylinder	Can you find the area of a <u>cylinder</u>?	cylinder
18.	fantastic	His <u>fantastic</u> singing voice could be heard from inside the building.	fantastic
19.	phantom	Have you read the legend of the <u>phantom</u> that rides a horse at night?	phantom
20.	physical	I'm taking <u>physical</u> education in school.	physical
21.	telephone	Did you hear the <u>telephone</u> ring?	telephone
22.	bowled	Have you ever <u>bowled</u> a strike?	bowled
23.	road	They live down the <u>road</u> from us.	road
24.	oar	Grab the <u>oar</u> and help me row the boat.	oar
25.	or	You may ride with them <u>or</u> ride with us.	or
26.	know	I <u>know</u> his brother very well.	know
27.	dough	There is enough <u>dough</u> for two loaves of bread.	dough
28.	hare	The tortoise beat the <u>hare</u> in the race.	hare
29.	pear	I brought a <u>pear</u> in my lunch.	pear
30.	border	We crossed the <u>border</u> into Mexico.	border

ALTERNATE LIFEPAC TEST

1.	banner	We hung a banner in front of our house, welcoming home mom and our new baby.	banner
2.	castle	One of the chess pieces is called a castle.	castle
3.	filled	My heart filled with joy when I heard that God loves me no matter what.	filled
4.	ghost	I just read a funny book about a friendly ghost.	ghost
5.	knife	That knife is not very sharp.	knife
6.	muscle	It took some muscle to push the car to the gas station.	muscle
7.	pneumonia	People with pneumonia are very ill.	pneumonia
8.	scenery	The mountain scenery was beautiful!	scenery
9.	boarder	A boarder is someone who rents one room of a house to live in.	boarder
10.	celery	I like to eat celery with my lunch.	celery
11.	celestial	Stars are celestial bodies.	celestial
12.	compliment	We should compliment each other often.	compliment
13.	citizen	I am a citizen of the United States of America.	citizen
14.	cough	My little sister has a bad cough when she is sick.	cough
15.	cylinder	Sometimes we call a basketball hoop a cylinder?	cylinder
16.	enough	Eating three meals is enough for one day.	enough
17.	frequent	Her frequent visits to her aunt make her aunt very happy.	frequent
18.	phantom	A phantom is alot like a ghost.	phantom
19.	physical	Chess is a mental, not physical, type of game.	physical
20.	telephone	In our house, we use the telephone quite a bit.	telephone
21.	bold	He was bold to tell them of Jesus.	bold
22.	bowled	I was bowled over by the surprising news.	bowled
23.	rode	She rode her horse everyday.	rode
24.	no	Is there no way to go through the mountains?	no
25.	peel	It is hard to peel an apple.	peel
26.	doe	The doe and her fawn moved quietly through the forest.	doe
27.	pair	I usually wear a pair of pants, a pair of socks, and a pair of shoes.	pair
28.	hair	I like the way he cut my hair.	hair
29.	peal	Hear the bells peal?	peal
30.	stationary	An anchor will keep a boat stationary.	stationary

LIFEPAC TEST

1. enjoyment — Playing guitar in church gave him a great deal of enjoyment. — enjoyment
2. excitement — After the choir sang, the congregation was filled with excitement. — excitement
3. amazement — The pastor stood in amazement after the powerful music had been presented. — amazement
4. achievement — Developing a cure for the disease was a great achievement. — achievement
5. swordless — The fallen knight was swordless. — swordless
6. advancement — The creation of the computer microchip was a technological advancement. — advancement
7. sleepless — Have aching legs at night ever made you sleepless? — sleepless
8. brimless — The hat he wore was brimless. — brimless
9. artist — Leonardo da Vinci was an inventor and an artist. — artist
10. ticklish — Are your feet ticklish? — ticklish
11. mannish — The hat has a mannish design. — mannish
12. fourth — I had the fourth highest test score. — fourth
13. eighth — The elevator took us to the eighth floor. — eighth
14. ninth — I am usually the ninth batter on the baseball team. — ninth
15. twentieth — We are going on our vacation on the twentieth of December. — twentieth
16. hundredth — That is the hundredth time he was late. — hundredth
17. materialism — The pastor spoke on the evils of materialism. — materialism
18. Americanism — A devotion or loyalty to the United States is called Americanism. — Americanism
19. baptism — I watched a beautiful baptism on Sunday. — baptism
20. Catholicism — Catholicism is one of the world's leading religions. — Catholicism
21. Communism — Communism is the form of government practiced in China. — Communism
22. nationalism — Nationalism means patriotic feelings or pride in your country. — nationalism
23. realism — The book was about realism. — realism
24. witticism — He is well known for his witticism. — witticism
25. anti-aircraft — The ship was equipped with anti-aircraft radar. — anti-aircraft
26. antibiotic — An antibiotic is a medicine that kills germs. — antibiotic
27. antichrist — Our pastor told us about the antichrist. — antichrist

LIFEPAC TEST cont...

28.	antifreeze	You know that there is a hole in your radiator if there is a puddle of antifreeze underneath the car.	antifreeze
29.	antiseptic	Hospitals sometimes have an antiseptic smell.	antiseptic
30.	antitoxin	The laboratory prepared the antitoxin.	antitoxin
31.	confront	I will confront him with the evidence.	confront
32.	program	The program listed all the participants.	program
33.	promise	Julie made a promise to be there.	promise
34.	unfair	The teacher was never unfair to his students.	unfair
35.	unwanted	No one desires to be unwanted.	unwanted
36.	employment	Dad had to work hard to find new employment.	employment
37.	bicyclist	The winner of the Tour de France bike race. was a great bicyclist.	bicyclist
38.	antidote	Milk is an antidote for some poisons.	antidote
39.	antisocial	John was considered antisocial because he didn't come to the party.	antisocial
40.	progress	By working hard, the student made much progress in her studies.	progress

ALTERNATE LIFEPAC TEST

1.	enjoyment	His main enjoyment was painting.	enjoyment
2.	excitement	The gift added to my excitement.	excitement
3.	amazement	Sam was filled with amazement at the sight.	amazement
4.	achievement	Developing a cure for the disease was a great achievement.	achievement
5.	employment	John's employment began last month.	employment
6.	advancement	He requested an advancement in pay.	advancement
7.	helpless	The small child was helpless.	helpless
8.	borderless	We bought the borderless wallpaper.	borderless
9.	scientist	When Jim grows up, he wants to be a scientist.	scientist
10.	bicyclist	The bicyclist made a trip across town.	bicyclist
11.	foolish	It is foolish to think it will happen.	foolish
12.	fourth	John was the fourth boy in line.	fourth
13.	fifth	Twenty cents is a fifth of a dollar.	fifth
14.	eighth	Jill is in the eighth grade.	eighth
15.	ninth	I live in the ninth house from the corner.	ninth
16.	twelfth	My birthday is on the twelfth of June.	twelfth
17.	twentieth	The twentieth of October is tomorrow.	twentieth
18.	fortieth	That couple is celebrating their fortieth anniversary.	fortieth
19.	materialism	The pastor spoke on the evils of materialism.	materialism
20.	Americanism	A devotion or loyalty to the United States is called Americanism.	Americanism
21.	baptism	The church will have a baptism on Sunday.	baptism
22.	Catholicism	Catholicism is one of the world's leading religions.	Catholicism
23.	heroism	He was rewarded for his heroism.	heroism
24.	nationalism	The spirit of nationalism is spreading.	nationalism
25.	organism	The human body is a complex organism.	organism
26.	antibiotic	The antibiotic will help him get over his illness.	antibiotic
27.	antichrist	Our pastor told us about the antichrist.	antichrist
28.	antidote	This is the antidote for the poison.	antidote
29.	antitrust	The antitrust bill was passed into law.	antitrust
30.	antisocial	Antisocial behavior is often just shyness.	antisocial
31.	confirm	Please confirm our reservation for lunch.	confirm
32.	context	My statement was taken out of context.	context
33.	progress	Wagon trains made slow progress across the desert.	progress

ALTERNATE LIFEPAC TEST cont...

34.	unguarded	The sheherd never leaves his sheep unguarded	unguarded
35.	restless	During the storm the dog seemed restless.	restless
36.	sleepless	Elizabeth had a sleepless night.	sleepless
37.	artist	The artist drew a picture of the sunset.	artist
38.	ticklish	My brother is ticklish.	ticklish
39.	antifreeze	My father put antifreeze in the car.	antifreeze
40.	antiseptic	Iodine is a widely used antiseptic.	antiseptic

LIFEPAC TEST

1.	addition	Tom passed the addition test.	addition
2.	attraction	I climbed a tree to see the attraction.	attraction
3.	celebration	The pastor led the Easter celebration.	celebration
4.	separation	After a long separation, we met.	separation
5.	supposition	He spoke to the class with the supposition that they would understand his message.	supposition
6.	afterward	He went to see the game afterward.	afterward
7.	forward	The army marched forward.	forward
8.	toward	The bird dove toward the ground.	toward
9.	beauteous	Another word for beautiful is beauteous.	beauteous
10.	fabulous	Bill and Cindy had a fabulous time at camp.	fabulous
11.	malicious	Becky refused to spread the malicious rumor.	malicious
12.	scandalous	That newspaper contains scandalous stories.	scandalous
13.	apprenticeship	Ralph needed to complete his apprenticeship.	apprenticeship
14.	authorship	He chose authorship as his profession.	authorship
15.	governorship	He wanted the governorship.	governorship
16.	kinship	My cousin and I have kinship?	kinship
17.	relationship	We have a new relationship to God through Jesus Christ.	relationship
18.	burdensome	Without Jesus' help, our troubles are too burdensome	burdensome
19.	quarrelsome	My sister and I are very quarrelsome.	quarrelsome
20.	loathesome	He had a loathesome picture.	loathesome
21.	toothsome	The pasta was toothsome.	toothsome
22.	winsome	He wrote in a winsome way.	winsome
23.	halves	A football game has two halves.	halves
24.	shelves	Books look good on shelves.	shelves
25.	thieves	Thieves take things that are not theirs.	thieves
26.	wives	They took their wives to dinner.	wives
27.	chiefs	They call their team the Chiefs.	chiefs
28.	handkerchiefs	Cowboys use handkerchiefs out on the trail.	handkerchiefs
29.	echoes	The sound echoes through the canyon.	echoes
30.	potatoes	French fries are made out of potatoes.	potatoes
31.	tomatoes	I always have tomatoes on my hamburgers.	tomatoes
32.	altos	We have two altos in the choir.	altos
33.	Eskimos	I just read a great book about Eskimos.	Eskimos
34.	pianos	All of the pianos were on sale.	pianos
35.	sopranos	Sopranos sing the higher notes.	sopranos

ALTERNATE LIFEPAC TEST

1.	attraction	The main attraction at the zoo was the lions.	attraction
2.	celebration	We are going to the birthday celebration.	celebration
3.	separation	Sin caused a separation between mankind and God.	separation
4.	vacation	She is going on vacation tomorrow.	vacation
5.	backward	He took two steps backward.	backward
6.	homeward	They are homeward bound.	homeward
7.	westward	The pioneers moved westward.	westward
8.	cautious	Be cautious when you cross the street.	cautious
9.	malicious	That boy is very malicious.	malicious
10.	scandalous	We heard some scandalous news.	scandalous
11.	suspicious	They were suspicious of the strange man.	suspicious
12.	apprenticeship	He did his apprenticeship with a plumbing company.	apprenticeship
13.	friendship	They had a good friendship.	friendship
14.	hardship	Trials and hardship will come.	hardship
15.	penmanship	Your penmanship has improved.	penmanship
16.	statesmanship	Do you have good statesmanship?	statesmanship
17.	burdensome	Let me take that burdensome load.	burdensome
18.	frolicsome	The cat was very frolicsome.	frolicsome
19.	quarrelsome	He is a quarrelsome person.	quarrelsome
20.	handsome	He is a very handsome person.	handsome
21.	lonesome	She is lonesome for her parents.	lonesome
22.	threesome	They make an interesting threesome.	threesome
23.	halves	Cut the cake into halves.	halves
24.	shelves	Let us fill the shelves with some glasses.	shelves
25.	thieves	The thieves were sentenced to prison.	thieves
26.	beliefs	Their beliefs in God were different than ours.	beliefs
27.	dwarfs	Dwarfs and elves are imaginary creatures.	dwarfs
28.	handkerchiefs	She has some beautiful handkerchiefs.	handkerchiefs
29.	proofs	The photographer showed them proofs of pictures taken at the wedding.	proofs
30.	heroes	The heroes returned from the war.	heroes
31.	potatoes	The farmer grows potatoes.	potatoes
32.	tomatoes	We like tomatoes.	tomatoes
33.	Eskimos	Eskimos live in Alaska.	Eskimos
34.	solos	She did two solos for the concert.	solos
35.	sopranos	How many sopranos are in the choir?	sopranos

LIFEPAC TEST

1.	laugh	The girl tried to laugh.	laugh
2	bough	The bough snapped when it was struck by lightning.	bough
3.	rough	The terrain was very rough for our climb.	rough
4.	dough	We made the dough for the cinnamon rolls.	dough
5.	thorough	Be thorough in your work.	thorough
6.	brief	The story was brief.	brief
7.	grief	Jesus helps people in time of grief.	grief
8.	limb	The limb of the tree bent during the wind storm.	limb
9.	pierce	The sound of the cymbal will pierce your ears.	pierce
10.	weapon	David used his sling as a weapon against Goliath.	weapon
11.	cite	A policeman will cite you for speeding.	cite
12.	knight	The knight was rewarded for his heroism.	knight
13.	night	Some animals only come out at night.	night
14.	sighs	Many sighs were heard as the winner was announced.	sighs
15.	pries	A detective pries into many areas to solve a case.	pries
16.	higher	I can jump higher than you.	higher
17.	idle	My car will idle roughly when it is cold.	idle
18.	idol	It is sinful to worship an idol.	idol
19.	isle	The crew was shipwrecked on an uncharted isle.	isle
20.	pried	The gopher pried through the dirt after his tunnel collapsed.	pried
21.	minor	Jerry had a minor cut on his knee.	minor
22.	fined	Alan was fined for returning his library book late.	fined
23.	find	I did not find my ball.	find
24.	caught	Bobby caught the fly ball and saved the baseball game.	caught
25.	fought	The committee fought hard to achieve its goals.	fought
26.	naughty	My puppy was naughty.	naughty
27.	sought	The President sought to end all wars.	sought
28.	thoughtful	It was so thoughtful of you to come visit me.	thoughtful
29.	conquer	Jesus can help you conquer your fears.	conquer

LIFEPAC TEST cont...

30.	emperor	The emperor of ancient China ruled an entire lifetime.	emperor
31.	restaurant	After Bible study, our group went to a restaurant for hot chocolate.	restaurant
32.	stallion	The beautiful stallion was fast.	stallion
33.	vacuum	The vacuum cleaner is broken.	vacuum
34.	worship	Every day, I worship my Lord.	worship
35.	chute	Please put your clothes down the chute.	chute
36.	decision	It was my own decision not to go on the trip.	decision
37.	emotion	No emotion was shown during the event.	emotion
38.	insure	Father will insure our new house in case of fire.	insure
39.	lotion	Before going out in the sun, put on some lotion so you do not burn.	lotion
40.	measure	We must measure the window before we buy new curtains.	measure
41.	pressure	When diving, you must allow enough time on your ascent for the pressure to change.	pressure
42.	solution	The solution to the problem is quite simple.	solution
43.	surely	Surely goodness and mercy shall follow me all the days of my life.	surely
44.	vacation	Our vacation this year will be a trip to Alaska.	vacation
45.	vision	Having a vision check is very important.	vision

ALTERNATE LIFEPAC TEST

1.	throughout	I slept throughout the plane ride.	throughout
2.	drought	The drought brought much hardship to the farmers.	drought
3.	tough	The geography test was tough.	tough
4.	doughnut	Would you like to eat a doughnut?	doughnut
5.	through	We went through the museum and saw many interesting exhibits.	through
6.	assign	It is your teacher's job to assign homework.	assign
7.	embarrass	Do not embarrass Frank in front of his friends.	embarrass
8.	kerchief	He lost his kerchief.	kerchief
9.	neigh	I heard my pony neigh when I approached the barn.	neigh
10.	shriek	The shriek of the train whistle startled me.	shriek
11.	sight	The sunset was a beautiful sight.	sight
12.	night	Some animals only came out at night.	night
13.	sighs	When his team lost, Jerry could not stop his sighs of dissapointment.	sighs
14.	size	What size shoe do you wear?	size
15.	prize	Did you win a prize?	prize
16.	hire	Father is going to hire an extra hand for the ranch.	hire
17.	idol	Some people treat a hero as an idol.	idol
18.	isle	The crew was shipwrecked on an uncharted isle.	isle
19.	aisle	There was an accident in the grocery aisle today.	aisle
20.	pried	We had to be careful as we pried open the wooden crate.	pried
21.	pride	As Christians we should be careful about our pride.	pride
22.	miner	My grandfather was a miner in Shamokin, Pennsylvania.	miner
23.	minor	Baseball players usually start in the minor leagues.	minor
24.	find	Did you help your mom find her car keys?	find
25.	bought	Aunt May bought me a hamster for my birthday.	bought
26.	cough	My daughter has a bad cough.	cough
27.	naught	She was dismayed to find that her efforts were for naught.	naught

ALTERNATE LIFEPAC TEST cont...

28.	slaughter	Yesterday, we watched the Cubs slaughter the Pirates.	slaughter
29.	taught	Our mother and father have taught us right from wrong.	taught
30.	biscuit	I love to eat butter on my biscuit.	biscuit
31.	disguise	Sally wore a disguise to school today for the Halloween party.	disguise
32.	physical	A physical fitness program will keep your body in shape.	physical
33.	rhythm	The rhythm of the verse made the poem more interesting.	rhythm
34.	vacuum	The vacuum cleaner is broken.	vacuum
35.	worship	I will worship the Lord with my whole heart.	worship
36.	chef	The chef prepared a beautiful and delicious meal.	chef
37.	confusion	In the midst of all the confusion, I did not hear your name.	confusion
38.	education	Education is an important part of your life.	education
39.	fiction	The story of Huckleberry Finn is a good example of fiction.	fiction
40.	issue	I just bought the latest issue of that comic book series.	issue
41.	machinery	The use of machinery has contributed to the planting and harvesting of crops.	machinery
42.	mission	While on their mission, the missionaries helped many people.	mission
43.	solution	I thought long and hard to find a solution.	solution
44.	suspicious	I was suspicious as I walked silently into the room.	suspicious
45.	vicious	The vicious lion roared at the zebra.	vicious

LIFEPAC TEST

1.	closure	The snow forced the closure of major roads.	closure
2.	failure	The electricity failure caused a city-wide blackout.	failure
3.	legislature	The legislature will pass the bill today.	legislature
4.	measure	Let's repeat the last measure of the song.	measure
5.	moisture	Moisture started to gather on the ground.	moisture
6.	pressure	The water pressure caused the pipe to explode.	pressure
7.	rapture	The little girl gazed in rapture at the circus.	rapture
8.	stature	Luke 2:52 says "Jesus grew in stature."	stature
9.	carriage	The carriage pulled in front of a large, white mansion.	carriage
10.	illusion	A magician uses illusion to fool the audience.	illusion
11.	intercession	The man's intercession stopped the argument.	intercession
12.	marriage	Marriage is an important part of life.	marriage
13.	stoppage	The work stoppage caused many problems.	stoppage
14.	supervision	Our hiking trip was under the supervision of Pastor Falconer.	supervision
15.	vain	"Thou shalt not take the name of the Lord thy God in vain."	vain
16.	wade	I love to wade in the creek.	wade
17.	waist	The water in the creek was up to my waist.	waist
18.	wait	Wait for me after class please, Sue.	wait
19.	way	There is only one way to be forgiven for your sins.	way
20.	weigh	Weigh the good and the bad before you make your decision.	weigh
21.	weighed	The package weighed four pounds.	weighed
22.	burial	Christ's burial in the tomb was the beginning for mankind.	burial
23.	comical	The two puppies playing together were a comical sight.	comical
24.	congressional	A congressional act is required to change law.	congressional
25.	editorial	The editorial concerned the massive flooding.	editorial
26.	electrical	The electrical outlet must be replaced.	electrical
27.	eventual	The eventual result was victory.	eventual
28.	industrial	A new industrial park is being built in our town.	industrial

LIFEPAC TEST cont...

| 29. | <u>musical</u> | The <u>musical</u> program at church was beautiful. | <u>musical</u> |
| 30. | <u>spiritual</u> | My <u>spiritual</u> life has grown a lot in the past year. | <u>spiritual</u> |

ALTERNATE LIFEPAC TEST

1. exposure — Exposure to the sun over a long period will cause a sunburn. — exposure
2. fracture — Daniel's fracture was the result of a fall. — fracture
3. literature — You may obtain good Christian literature at the church. — literature
4. mixture — The mixture of yellow and red paint creates an orange color. — mixture
5. pleasure — The Easter concert gave us much pleasure. — pleasure
6. procedure — The assembly procedure was shown on the box. — procedure
7. Scripture — The Scripture foretold the coming of a Saviour. — Scripture
8. structure — The structure burned to the ground. — structure
9. allusion — He was hurt by their allusion to his poor sportsmanship. — allusion
10. conclusion — My conclusion proved correct. — conclusion
11. intercession — The man's intercession stopped the argument. — intercession
12. shrinkage — Be careful of shrinkage when washing your clothes. — shrinkage
13. storage — We got our furniture out of storage. — storage
14. usage — Good usage of language is a fine quality in a person. — usage
15. vein — The vein in the gold mine was extensive. — vein
16. waist — The water in the creek was up to my waist. — waist
17. wait — Wait for me after class, please, Sue. — wait
18. waste — Do not waste food because many people in the world are hungry. — waste
19. way — There is only one way to be forgiven for your sins. — way
20. weigh — Weigh the good and the bad before you make your decision. — weigh
21. weight — The weight that Christ carried to the cross was a heavy burden. — weight
22. clerical — The error was clearly clerical. — clerical
23. commercial — We must strive to make Christmas less commercial. — commercial
24. contractual — This fulfills our contractual agreement. — contractual
25. electrical — The electrical outlet must be replaced. — electrical
26. financial — Due to financial difficulties, the play was canceled. — financial
27. intellectual — My professor is highly intellectual. — intellectual
28. presidential — The presidential election will be held in November. — presidential
29. racial — We can be proud of the racial equality that we have achieved. — racial
30. spiritual — My spiritual life has grown a lot in the past year. — spiritual

LIFEPAC TEST

1.	abandon	As Christians we should never abandon hope in Christ.	abandon
2.	abroad	Peter and Rusty will travel abroad this summer.	abroad
3.	abrupt	The story came to an abrupt end.	abrupt
4.	account	On account of her poor grades, Stephanie was assigned a tutor.	account
5.	adopt	Jody wants to adopt the puppy.	adopt
6.	allow	Do not allow yourself to be lead into temptation.	allow
7.	apparent	It was apparent that the storm was approaching.	apparent
8.	apprentice	The apprentice carpenter hit his thumb instead of the nail.	apprentice
9.	aquarium	The aquarium contained many exotic tropical fish.	aquarium
10.	attach	Attach the memo to the bulletin board, please.	attach
11.	broadside	Our car was hit broadside in the parking lot.	broadside
12.	fireplace	A mantle stretched the entire length of the fireplace.	fireplace
13.	grapevine	The grapevine grew up the trellis rapidly.	grapevine
14.	hardship	The search team experienced undue hardship.	hardship
15.	puppet	The children enjoyed the puppet show that depicted the nativity.	puppet
16.	rascal	Johnny surely is a mischievous rascal!	rascal
17.	reptile	A copperhead snake is a reptile.	reptile
18.	rugged	The mountains were rugged and difficult to climb.	rugged
19.	teammate	Our teammate was selected for the all-star team.	teammate
20.	witness	Just as Christ shared the good news, so should we witness to others around us.	witness
21.	alley	The alley runs behind our house.	alley
22.	battle	David won the battle against Goliath with only a slingshot.	battle
23.	clothes	The clothes are not dry yet.	clothes
24.	crumble	The cliff began to crumble as a result of the tremor.	crumble
25.	delight	I delight to do my Father's will.	delight
26.	exercise	Exercise is good for your muscle tone.	exercise

LIFEPAC TEST cont...

27.	fatal	A fall from this height would prove fatal.	fatal
28.	guard	Pilate placed a guard at the tomb.	guard
29.	guide	The guide showed us through the museum.	guide
30.	hospital	Sylvester is in the hospital having his tonsils taken out.	hospital

ALTERNATE LIFEPAC TEST

1.	hymn	My favorite hymn is "The Old Rugged Cross."	hymn
2.	jersey	He ripped his baseball jersey sliding into third base.	jersey
3.	midnight	The train was scheduled to arrive at midnight.	midnight
4.	nickel	Many years ago, a hot dog cost only a nickel.	nickel
5.	pleasant	We had a pleasant time at the picnic.	pleasant
6.	president	The president played golf on vacation.	president
7.	suppose	I suppose I'd better get changed.	suppose
8.	valley	The valley was covered with beautiful daffodils.	valley
9.	wrist	Jennifer broke her wrist while tobogganing.	wrist
10.	wrong	I was in the wrong place when my friends came to pick me up.	wrong
11.	beach	We roasted hot dogs on the beach.	beach
12.	beech	The beech tree swayed fiercely during the storm.	beech
13.	creak	The floor will continue to creak unless it is fixed.	creak
14.	creek	The creek was so crystal clear you could see the bottom, even in eight feet of water.	creek
15.	flea	Last Saturday we went to the flea market.	flea
16.	flee	Lot and his family were told to flee from Sodom.	flee
17.	feat	Charles was awarded for his tremendous feat.	feat
18.	feet	My new sneakers hurt my feet.	feet
19.	knead	Sally helped her grandmother knead the dough.	knead
20.	need	The need to spread the Gospel is great.	need
21.	peace	Peace was finally established between the countries.	peace
22.	piece	Sarah gave me a piece of her birthday cake.	piece
23.	peal	The peal of the church bells was heard throughout the town.	peal
24.	peel	The soldier had to peel the potatoes for the weekend meals.	peel
25.	peer	A peer is someone of the same rank.	peer
26.	pier	The boat hit the pier.	pier
27.	real	Christ is a real friend to all.	real
28.	reel	The reel broke just as I caught a huge fish.	reel

ALTERNATE LIFEPAC TEST cont...

29. <u>steal</u>   The eighth commandment is "Thou shalt not <u>steal</u>."   <u>steal</u>
30. <u>steel</u>   The <u>steel</u> file cabinet will arrive next week.   <u>steel</u>

LIFEPAC TEST

1.	abound	In Alaska, fish and bears abound.	abound
2.	boiling	Put the eggs in when the water is boiling.	boiling
3.	caution	The driver of the speeding car disregarded the caution sign.	caution
4.	coward	Just because you do not fight does not mean you are a coward.	coward
5.	failure	Tom's failure did not discourage him.	failure
6.	mistake	Do not give up when you make a mistake.	mistake
7.	praying	The preacher knelt in his office, praying for the coming service.	praying
8.	royal	The peasant turned out to be his royal highness, Prince Richard.	royal
9.	suppose	Do you suppose they will visit again next year?	suppose
10.	tower	Old castles often have a tower at each corner.	tower
11.	advance	This year I will advance to the ninth grade.	advance
12.	available	Marc is available whenever you need him.	available
13.	discourage	Sammy tried to discourage her from making a hasty decision.	discourage
14.	exceedingly	I am exceedingly glad that you are coming with us.	exceedingly
15.	fiction	A make-believe story is fiction.	fiction
16.	glisten	The dewdrops glisten in the early morning light.	glisten
17.	leadership	Ken learned about leadership qualities from his father.	leadership
18.	sigh	Lee gave a big sigh of relief as he turned in his test.	sigh
19.	wrestle	Harvey liked to wrestle with his dad.	wrestle
20.	brand-new	Dawn got a brand-new bat for her birthday.	brand-new
21.	childhood	I had a wonderful childhood in northern Michigan.	childhood
22.	haven't	I haven't seen Kathy all day.	haven't
23.	landscape	The teacher showed them how to paint a landscape.	landscape
24.	separate	We counted off to separate into teams.	separate
25.	should've	I should've tried harder to help.	should've
26.	you're	I know you're tired, but we have to keep going.	you're
27.	compliment	Most people like to receive a compliment now and then.	compliment

LIFEPAC TEST cont...

28.	fantastic	The space ride at the amusement park is <u>fantastic</u>.	fantastic
29.	muscle	Randy pulled a <u>muscle</u> during the race.	muscle
30.	oar	Pete dropped the <u>oar</u> over the side of the boat.	oar
31.	pear	Beverly had a <u>pear</u> for lunch.	pear
32.	Americanism	A devotion or loyalty to the United States is <u>Americanism</u>.	Americanism
33.	antichrist	An <u>antichrist</u> is someone against Christ.	antichrist
34.	fortieth	Mom and Dad are celebrating their <u>fortieth</u> anniversary.	fortieth
35.	afterward	We will go to dinner <u>afterward</u>.	afterward
36.	burdensome	His constant complaining is <u>burdensome</u>.	burdensome
37.	celebration	We planned a <u>celebration</u> in honor of his return.	celebration
38.	relationship	Tom's <u>relationship</u> to Christ has grown in the last few weeks.	relationship
39.	drought	The <u>drought</u> created many hardships on the people.	drought
40.	minor	Juliet has a <u>minor</u> in music.	minor
41.	literature	Our <u>literature</u> class is reading the Psalms.	literature
42.	Scripture	Whenever I have a problem, I turn to God and <u>Scripture</u>.	Scripture
43.	supervision	Adult <u>supervision</u> is important on field trips.	supervision
44.	waste	Suzanne, do not <u>waste</u> your time.	waste
45.	weigh	Before making a decision, <u>weigh</u> all sides.	weigh
46.	apparent	The empty seats showed an <u>apparent</u> lack of interest.	apparent
47.	exercise	The best way to stay healthy is to <u>exercise</u>.	exercise
48.	nickel	When I was a child, candy cost one cent— not a <u>nickel</u>.	nickel
49.	steal	Steve will <u>steal</u> second base if he can.	steal
50.	teammate	Our <u>teammate</u> hurt himself playing ball.	teammate

ALTERNATE LIFEPAC TEST

1.	arrange	I can arrange to meet you at three o'clock.	arrange
2.	freedom	We have freedom of religion in the United States.	freedom
3.	mountain	I love hiking in the mountain range north of here.	mountain
4.	voyage	Columbus made a voyage to the New World.	voyage
5.	encourage	My teammates encourage me to try again when I make an error.	encourage
6.	afternoon	Saturday afternoon we are going on a picnic to the lake.	afternoon
7.	business	My father's business partner is coming to dinner.	business
8.	she'll	I hope she'll be on time to the meeting.	she'll
9.	we'd	We'd better go home now.	we'd
10.	won't	Are you sure you won't have some more ice cream?	won't
11.	you've	John, you've got a fly on your nose!	you've
12.	celery	A stalk of celery is almost all water.	celery
13.	citizen	I am a citizen of the United States.	citizen
14.	cough	Teri has a cold and a bad cough.	cough
15.	knife	I could not find a clean knife in the house.	knife
16.	or	Do you want to play football or baseball?	or
17.	pair	I got a pair of skates for my birthday.	pair
18.	amazement	Angela gazed in amazement at the beauty of the Grand Canyon.	amazement
19.	eighth	Johnny was eighth in the race.	eighth
20.	employment	Anne was offered employment at the space center.	employment
21.	enjoyment	It gives me enjoyment to be with you.	enjoyment
22.	fortieth	Mom and Dad are celebrating their fortieth anniversary.	fortieth
23.	progress	Betty made rapid progress in math.	progress
24.	scientist	The scientist discovered a new form of energy.	scientist
25.	authorship	Who questions the authorship of this novel?	authorship
26.	cautious	Patty was cautious as she approached the edge of the ravine.	cautious
27.	echoes	We created countless echoes as we hiked through the canyon.	echoes
28.	fabulous	Paul, the shortstop, made a fabulous catch.	fabulous

ALTERNATE LIFEPAC TEST cont...

29.	halves	Kathy divided the apple into halves.	halves
30.	heroes	There were many heroes during World War II.	heroes
31.	quarrelsome	The dog and cat appeared to be in quarrelsome moods.	quarrelsome
32.	cite	The officer will cite you for littering.	cite
33.	conquer	David was able to conquer Goliath because he trusted God.	conquer
34.	idol	While Moses was on the mountain, the people below built an idol.	idol
35.	miner	My grandfather was a miner in Shamokin, PA.	miner
36.	rhythm	The rhythm of the drums could be heard for blocks.	rhythm
37.	tough	The team was tough to beat.	tough
38.	conclusion	The committee's conclusion was to support the missionary.	conclusion
39.	marriage	The marriage ceremony was held in the garden.	marriage
40.	spiritual	The spiritual song was very moving.	spiritual
41.	usage	The usage of the word was incorrect.	usage
42.	waist	The baseball uniform was too small in the waist.	waist
43.	way	We went the wrong way and wound up in Tortilla Flat.	way
44.	feat	The fireman was awarded a medal for his brave feat.	feat
45.	feet	My feet were soaked from the morning dew.	feet
46.	peace	World peace will be hard to accomplish.	peace
47.	piece	The model airplane was missing one piece.	piece
48.	puppet	A puppet show will be given for the children.	puppet
49.	steel	Many things we use each day are made from steel.	steel
50.	thieves	The thieves were caught in the park just after the robbery.	thieves

Notes

ALTERNATE

TESTS & KEYS

Reproducible Tests
for use with the Language Arts
500 Teacher's Guide

Name _____

Match these items (each answer, 4 points).

1. _____ language arts
2. _____ speaking and writing
3. _____ setting
4. _____ oi
5. _____ scribes
6. _____ phobia
7. _____ characters
8. _____ reading and listening

a. receiving information from others
b. Jewish teachers
c. fear
d. people in the story
e. students
f. common vowel diphthong
g. giving and receiving information
h. place or places where the story takes place
i. giving information to others

Complete these sentences (each answer, 4 points).

9. A vowel that is not sounded is called a _____ vowel.
10. A story told in conversation is a _____ .
11. The _____ marks are used to show how the vowels are pronounced.
12. A _____ gives you the meaning of many words.
13. The main events in a story are called the _____ .
14. Information arranged in the correct _____ of the events helps you to remember the information.
15. An author may state fact or _____ .
16. A _____ is a word that names a person, place, or thing.

Complete these items (each lettered answer, 2 points).

17. Write four vowel diphthongs.

    a. _____ as in_____   b. _____ as in_____
    c. _____ as in_____   d. _____ as in_____

18. Write four vowel digraphs.

    a. _____ as in_____   b. _____ as in_____
    c. _____ as in_____   d. _____ as in_____

Match these items (each answer, 2 points).

	Entry		Respelling
19.	_____ physical	a.	gal' u lē'
20.	_____ synagogue	b.	tùr
21.	_____ account	c.	dil' u junt
22.	_____ Galilee	d.	ad mīr
23.	_____ memorize	e.	bi hāv'
24.	_____ approximately	f.	u prok' su mit lē
25.	_____ behave	g.	u kount'
26.	_____ diligent	h.	fiz' u kul
27.	_____ admire	i.	sin' u gog
28.	_____ tour	j.	mem' u rīz
		k.	u par' unt lē

Date _____

Score _____

Possible Score _____ **100** _____

Name _____

Choose the correct word to complete the sentence (each answer, 2 points).

hyphen	sea	nouns	courage
adverbs	main idea	mood	topic
language arts	adjectives	summarize	paragraph

1.   The art of giving and receiving information is called _____
     _____ .

2.   The Polynesians worshiped _____ .

3.   Mafatu feared the _____ .

4.   The author uses emotion words to express a _____ .

5.   Some compound words are joined by a _____ .

6.   Telling *who* or *what* the paragraph is about, is giving the _____
     _____ .

7.   When an action is being described, the words that are used to answer the
     question "How?" are _____ .

8.   Sometimes the last sentence will "sum up" or _____ what was said.

9.   The sentence that gives the main idea is sometimes called the _____
     sentence.

10. Descriptive words are called _____ .

Write an example of each item (each answer, 3 points).

11. mood word   _____

12. a noun   _____

13. an adverb   _____

14. a contraction   _____

15. hyphenated compound   _____

16. hyphenated number word   _____

17. one-word compound   _____

18. two-word compound   _____

19. synonym for *speak*   _____

20. an *-ing* verb   _____

21. a word with consonant twins   _____

22. a spelling word that has *nut*   _____
     in the middle

Complete these items (each answer, 5 points).

23.   Write a statement of fact from the "The Flight." _____

_____

24.   Write a statement of opinion from the "The Flight." _____

_____

_____

Write *true* or *false* (each answer, 2 points).

25. _____ The author of *Call It Courage* is Armstrong Sperry.
26. _____ The name of the albatross was Uri.
27. _____ A lagoon is a small body of water connected to a larger body of water.
28. _____ The Polynesians in *Call It Courage* were fishermen.
29. _____ Mafatu's dog was a bulldog.
30. _____ Mafatu's mother was killed by a hurricane when he was three years old.
31. _____ Kivi guided Mafatu out into the open ocean.

Match these items (each answer, 2 points).

32. _____ consonant twins   a. feelings
33. _____ folk hero   b. contraction
34. _____ diamante   c. compound word
35. _____ resentment   d. two consonants
36. _____ moods   e. Moana
37. _____ pandanas mat   f. describing word
38. _____ book   g. a feeling resulting from insult
39. _____ moonlight   h. Mafatu
40. _____ they're   i. *Call It Courage*
41. _____ adjective   j. floor covering
     k. a kind of poem

Date _____
Score _____
Possible Score _____ 100 _____

Name _____

Answer *true* or *false* (each answer, 1 point).

1. _____ God talked to man in the garden of Eden.
2. _____ A summary is a long explanation.
3. _____ An author only writes to influence your thinking.
4. _____ The main idea is a summary of all the details found in a certain paragraph or reading selection.
5. _____ Over the years the English language has remained the same.
6. _____ A time line shows the order in which events have occurred in history.
7. _____ Idioms are phrases with meanings that cannot be understood from the ordinary meaning of words.
8. _____ Adverbs describe nouns.
9. _____ Antonyms are words that are spelled the same but have different meanings.
10. _____ The *effect* is the result of the *cause*.

Number the events from Genesis, Chapter 3, Verse 1 through 8, in the proper order (each event, 3 points).

11. _____ Adam and Eve hid from God.
12. _____ Eve told the serpent that God said not to eat of the tree in the middle of the garden or they would die.
13. _____ Adam and Eve heard the voice of God.
14. _____ The serpent said Adam and Eve would not die.
15. _____ Adam and Eve ate of the forbidden tree.

Circle the correct pronunciation for each heteronym (each answer, 3 points).

16. A strong *wind* blew down the old tree.
    wīnd   wind
17. The actor took a *bow* after his performance.
    bou   bō

Write an *S* on the line in front of each complete sentence and *NS* in front of each incomplete sentence (each item, 2 points).

18. _____ The history of language is very exciting.
19. _____ A new language to learn.
20. _____ God said His Word shall not pass away.

Draw one line under the subject and two lines under each predicate (each sentence, 3 points).

21. The two boys explored the cave.
22. The rare butterfly was caught in the net.

Draw one line under each cause and two lines under each effect (each sentence, 3 points).

23. The boy stayed out in the sun too long and received a severe sunburn.
24. A person can die from an inadequate supply of water.
25. With Jesus Christ in your life, you can have an abundant life.

Add a prefix or suffix to each root word to change or add to its meaning (each answer, 3 points).

26. _____common
27. joy_____
28. pain_____
29. comfort_____
30. _____perfect

Draw one line under each adjective and two lines under each adverb (each sentence, 2 points).

31. The pleasant gentleman spoke kindly to the boy.
32. The angry grocer quickly added up the purchase.
33. The couple ate often in the little cafe.

Match each homonym with its meaning (each answer, 2 points).

34. _____ paws   a. someone under age; not important
35. _____ pause   b. feet of an animal having claws
36. _____ minor   c. man who works in a mine
37. _____ miner   d. to stop for a short moment

Write a definition for each idiom (each definition, 5 points).

38.   When Sarah forgot her raincoat, she knew she was *in a jam*.

_____

39.   The school party got a little *out of hand*.

_____

Answer this question (this answer, 5 points).

40.   Why do people all over the world speak different languages?

_____

_____

_____

Name the type of propaganda technique used in this statement (this answer, 4 points).

41.   Our fruit drink contains more natural fruit juices than any other fruit drink.

_____

Date _____

Score _____

Possible Score _____ **100** _____

Name _____

Answer *true* or *false* (each answer, 2 points).

1. _____ Friendliness is a good character or personality trait.
2. _____ A main idea is always stated and never implied.
3. _____ The first step in writing a report is to select a topic.
4. _____ The words *space, shape, size, stroke,* and *slant* refer to personality traits.
5. _____ You should only gather report information from resource books.
6. _____ An opinion is a statement that tells what a person thinks or feels about a fact.
7. _____ A metaphor is a type of adverb.
8. _____ Note cards are helpful in organizing report information.
9. _____ Character traits are inferred by what the characters do and say.
10. _____ A simile is a kind of figurative language.

Read the following paragraphs. Then complete the activities that follow.

Putting out fires today is much different from what it was years ago. Years ago people had not heard of fire engines. The closest resemblance to a siren was someone yelling, "Fire!" or the clanging of a church bell. Then people would dash from their homes and form a bucket brigade. Buckets were filled with water and passed along the lines, to throw on the fire. This process was slow.

Today someone usually calls the fire department. Firefighters race to the fire in well-equipped trucks, hook up to a fire hydrant, and quickly put out the fire. The highly-trained firefighters use special equipment in order to reach and control fires better. Modern firefighting is a great improvement over the bucket brigade.

Draw a circle around the sentence that best gives the main idea of the paragraphs (this item, 3 points).

11. a. Firefighters put out fires quickly.
    b. Church bells make good fire alarms.
    c. Putting out fires today is much different than it was years ago.

Write one detail from the paragraphs which supports the main idea (this item, 3 points).

12. _____

Number the following events in proper order (each answer, 3 points).

13. _____ People dashed from their homes.

14. _____ The buckets of water were then passed along and thrown on the fire.

15. _____ Someone yelled, "Fire!" or rang a church bell.

16. _____ A bucket brigade was formed.

17. _____ Buckets were filled with water.

Put the items from the list in their correct places in the outline (each answer, 2 points).

> Putting out fires years ago
> Fire trucks hook up to fire hydrants
> People yelled, "Fire!" or rang church bells
> Putting out fires today
> A bucket brigade was formed

18. A. _____

19.   1. _____

20.   2. _____

    3. Buckets of water were passed to throw on the fire

21. B. _____

    1. People call the fire department

22.   2. _____

    3. Highly trained firemen and special equipment put out fires quickly

Write *F* on the blank if the sentence is a fact, and *O* if it is an opinion (each answer, 2 points).

23. _____ The United States is located in the Northern Hemisphere.

24. _____ The dress is beautiful.

25. _____ I think this is the best book on space.

26. _____ Water evaporates into vapor.

Write *S* if the sentence is a statement, *RC* for request or command, *E* for exclamation, and *Q* for a question. Put the correct punctuation mark at the end (each numbered item, 3 points).

27. a. _____ Stop thief b._____
28. a. _____ This city is the largest in the state b._____
29. a. _____ What is the largest planet in the solar system b._____
30. a. _____ Please open the door b._____

Draw one line under the subject and two lines under each predicate (each underline, 2 points).

31. The horses were harnessed to the plow.
32. The distant smoke signals relayed a message of trouble.

Write *ADJ* for adjective or *ADV* for adverb for each italicized word (each answer, 2 points).

33. the *blue* ocean
34. fought *bravely*
35. a *quiet* room
36. coming *soon*

Write *M* if the sentence contains a metaphor, and *S* if it contains a simile (each answer, 2 points).

37. _____ The slim boy is straight like an arrow.
38. _____ The angry man growled like a bear.
39. _____ He is a sly old fox.
40. _____ The glider was an eagle soaring through the air.

Read Genesis Chapter 4, Verses 1 though 8. Compare and contrast Cain and Abel (this item, 5 points).

41. _____
_____
_____
_____

Date _____
Score _____
Possible Score _____ 100 _____

Name _____

Write *true* or *false* (each answer, 2 points).

1. _____ A *summary* is a brief way of telling a story.
2. _____ One suffix that makes a noun from a verb is -*ment*.
3. _____ A *retinue* is the lord who has a right to homage.
4. _____ Seeing or writing about things as they really are is called *realism*.
5. _____ The *plot* is the place or places where the story happens.
6. _____ The person who follows another in a position is the *successor*.
7. _____ Antifreeze is a liquid with a low freezing point.
8. _____ A *seed idea* is a very small idea which is put into a story besides the main idea.
9. _____ The correct spelling of the ordinal number for five is *fiveth*.
10. _____ An implied meaning is one which can usually be understood from the context.

Write *G* for *good* and *P* for *poor* in front of each sentence (each answer, 2 points).

11. _____ Anyways, we all had a good time.
12. _____ You gave me less pieces than you gave Tim.
13. _____ Let me open the package for you.
14. _____ I hear you are doing well in your music studies.

Name the element of plot development each statement represents (each answer, 3 points).

15. _____ The story is about Tom, a sixth grader, his dog, Bruno, and a lost child.
16. _____ The story takes place in a wooded area near the farm where Tom lives.
17. _____ Tom and his dog have several adventures in the woods before they find the lost child and bring her back to her parents.

Match these items (each answer, 3 points).

18. _____	an iron block on which metals are hammered	a. Sir Ector
19. _____	a story that has come down from the past that many people have believed	b. anvil
20. _____	one of the elements of a story that adds to the pleasure of reading	c. characters' conversation
21. _____	the steward in charge of a royal palace	d. fable
22. _____	thought he might be king of Britain	e. seneschal
23. _____	took Arthur into his home and raised him	f. legend
24. _____	should sound the way people of that period talked	g. generosity
25. _____	a good characteristic of Sir Ector's	h. Sir Kay
26. _____	a poor characteristic of Arthur's	i. acting without thinking
27. _____	known for magic	j. Merlin
28. _____	combat between two knights	k. suspense
		l. jousting

Complete these items (each answer, 3 points).

29. List four of the six questions to ask yourself when judging the value of a story as literature.

   a. _____

   b. _____

   c. _____

   d. _____

On the line, write the letter from the list for who the speaker would be (each answer, 2 points).

   a. bully
   b. mother
   c. knight at King Arthur's court
   d. man at the counter of hamburger stand

30. _____ Okay, kid, wottlit be?
31. _____ Gimme at or I'll bustya one!
32. _____ Gladly will I serve you, my liege.
33. _____ Did you have a good day?

Number the sentences in the order they should be read (each answer, 2 points).

34. _____ Take cap off of crankcase.
35. _____ Unscrew nut from oil pan.
36. _____ Fill crankcase with oil to specified amount.
37. _____ Allow oil to drain.
38. _____ Screw nut back on to oil pan.

Date _____
Score _____
Possible Score _____100_____

Name _____

Match the words and phrases (each answer, 2 points).

1.	_____	what a poet writes rather than paragraphs	a. ballads
2.	_____	a rhythmical pattern that is not completely regular	b. rhymed quatrain
			c. emotion
3.	_____	writing or speaking about a thing as if it were a person	d. cadence
			e. personification
4.	_____	story poems that are sung	f. stanzas
5.	_____	two lines with the same beat and rhymed end words	g. stress
			h. rhymed couplet
6.	_____	things or happenings that stand for ideas	i. pen picture
7.	_____	four lines of poetry that have a rhyming pattern	j. symbols
			k. free verse
8.	_____	does not need to rhyme but must have a cadence	
9.	_____	beat or emphasis	
10.	_____	short poem of three lines, each line being a metaphor	

Write *true* or *false* (each answer, 2 points).

11. _____ Every poem must have rhythm.
12. _____ To get the most out of poetry, it should be read silently.
13. _____ A conundrum is an inspirational poem.
14. _____ A pun is a play on words.
15. _____ The simile and metaphor are types of poems.
16. _____ Emotion in a poem is made by rhythm alone.
17. _____ Poetry expresses strong feelings in a few words.
18. _____ A good choice of words makes the reader see pictures and share in whatever the poet sees and feels.
19. _____ Repetition of sounds is not used in poetry.
20. _____ Inspirational poetry is the kind that makes you want to be a better person.

Write the correct letter and answer on each line (each answer, 2 points).

21. From "Landing of the Pilgrim Fathers in New England," the phrase "stern and rock-bound coast" means_____ .
   a. welcoming place
   b. difficult landing place
   c. easy landing

22. From "Landing of Pilgrim Fathers in New England," the phrase "faith's pure shrine" means_____ .
   a. a place to worship according to their faith
   b. a landing place
   c. a place to live

23.   Rhythm is made by_____.
        a. rhyming words   b. poetic language   c. stressed syllables
24.   Slow rhythm and soft sounds belong to _____.
        a.   lullabies and other peaceful poems
        b.   patriotic ideas
        c.   humorous poems
25.   Ballads are usually_____.
        a.   in two-lines stanzas
        b.   in four-line stanzas
        c.   short
26.   "King John and the Abbot of Canterbury" is an example of _____
        _____.
        a.   an inspirational poem
        b.   a ballad
        c.   a limerick
27.   The idea taught in "King John and the Abbot of Canterbury" is that
        _____.
        a.   all shepherds are wiser than abbots or kings
        b.   humor can sometimes get you out of difficulty
        c.   dressing up like someone else is a way to earn money
28.   "As busy as a bee" is an example of a _____.
        a. metaphor   b. simile   c. couplet
29.   "A great lion of a warrior" is an example of a _____.
        a. metaphor   b. quatrain   c. simile
30.   In "the lonely hill discards the green smock she wore all summer," the
        words *green smock* stand for _____ .
        a. a fancy pin   b. feathers   c. grass

Choose the more poetic sentence of the pair of sentences (each answer, 3
points).
31.   _____ a. Amidst the storm they sang.
                    b. They sang in the middle of the storm.
32.   _____ a. The church spires stand up from rich meadows of corn.
                    b. Up from the meadows rich with corn, the cluster spires
                       stand.
33.   _____ a. The true-hearted did not come as the conqueror came.
                    b. Not as the conqueror comes, they, the true-hearted came.
34.   _____ a. The smith, a mighty man is he, with large and sinewy
                       hands.
                    b. The mighty village smith has large and sinewy hands.
35.   _____ a. And I'll tell you a story, a story so merry.
                    b. I'll tell you a merry story.

Underline the stress syllables in the following lines (each line, 3 points).

36.   A hundred men, as the king heard say.

37.   An ancient story I'll tell you anon.

38.   Under a spreading chestnut tree.

39.   I know that He abides with me.

40.   I do not know tomorrow's way.

Answer this question (each answer, 2 points).

41.   What are five things that can make poetry enjoyable?

     a.   _____

     b.   _____

     c.   _____

     d.   _____

     e.   _____

Date _____

Score _____

Possible Score _____ **100** _____

Name _____

Number each group of events in proper sequence (each answer, 2 points).

1. _____ The man took an inventory of Gulliver's pockets.
2. _____ The little people shot Gulliver with arrows.
3. _____ Gulliver found himself tied to the ground.

----

4. _____ Marc escaped to Seth's house.
5. _____ Marc went to live with the cave people.
6. _____ Marc and his family were put in prison.

Write the correct letter and answer on each line (each answer, 3 points).

7. Your reaction to getting a horse of your own would be _____ .
   a. sorrow   b. excitement   c. embarrassment

8. The main idea of the story, "A Voyage to Lilliput," is _____
   _____ .
   a. Gulliver, held by the little people, wants to be free.
   b. Gulliver wants to live with the little people.
   c. Gulliver wants to take the little people back to England.

9. *I tried to copy the answers from my friend's paper carefully. Then I noticed the teacher looking straight at me. I hung my head and my face turned bright red.*
   The mood of this paragraph is _____ .
   a. joy   b. shame   c. anger

10. Using Christian judgment, the right thing was done when _____
    _____ .
    a. The lady at the store gave Tom too much money and he kept it.
    b. In his disappointment, Sam wrote an angry note to his friend.
    c. Sally helped her mother when she was sick.

Answer these questions (each numbered item, 4 points).

11. In this sentence, "Peggy ate too much and now she feels sick," what is the cause and what is the effect?
    a. cause _____
    b. effect _____

12. What is the correct word order for this sentence? "The leaves tiny, yellow fell off the tree old."
    _____
    _____

13. Expand this basic sentence by adding two adjectives. "The tree stood in the meadow."
    _____
    _____

14. What event do you infer happened between these two events?
   a. Kelly watched the leaves fall off the tree. She decided to get the rake.
   b. Later, father wondered what happened to all the leaves.

   _____

   _____

15. Identify the noun that is the subject and the noun that is the object of the following sentence. "The boy made a sandwich."
   a. noun as subject _____
   b. noun as object _____

Match these items (each answer, 2 points).

16. _____ a great missionary   a. Matthew
17. _____ coal   b. Cyrenius
18. _____ teacher's   c. Paul
19 _____ twenty   d. common noun
20. _____ Alaska   e. proper noun
21. _____ we   f. possessive noun
22. _____ healthy   g. pronoun
23. _____ his   h. adjective
24. _____ Marc's older brother i. number adjective
25. _____ adopted Thad   j. possessive pronoun
                                  k. verb

Change the singular nouns to plural nouns and the plural nouns to their singular form (each answer, 2 points).

26. house   _____
27. geese   _____
28. toy   _____
29. babies _____
30. feet   _____
31. lady   _____

Match the words to their meanings (each answer, 2 points).

32 _____ detailed list of articles   a. potion
33. _____ shelter, protection   b. inventory
34. _____ person who is put to death or   c. martyr
           made to suffer greatly for his beliefs   d. refuge
35. _____ make clean   e. bitter
36. _____ a medicine or poison   f. debate
37. _____ talk about reasons for and against   g. shrill
38. _____ high sharp sound   h. purge

Write *0* if the sentence is an opinion and *F* if it is a fact (each answer, 2
points).

39. _____ George Washington was the first President of the United
States.
40. _____ I believe we will have a good winter this year.
41. _____ California is a state.
42. _____ Bob will probably win the race.
43. _____ A sunset is beautiful.

Date _____
Score _____
Possible Score _____ 100 _____

Language Arts 508 Alternate Test

Name _____

Match these items (each answer, 2 points).

1. _____	to get off a horse, bicycle, and so forth	a. action verb
2 _____	may be used as a main verb if a helping verb is used	b. participle
3. _____	changes its form without adding -ed to form the past tense	c. contraction
4 _____	tells what the subject is	d. adverb
5. _____	not real; imaginary, made-up characters	e. parable
6. _____	earthly story with a heavenly meaning	f. fable
7. _____	made by joining two words together and leaving out one or more letters	g. fictitious
8. _____	modifies a verb	h. dismount
9. _____	tells what the subject does	i. irregular
10. _____	short story that is meant to teach a lesson	j. complete sentence
		k. verb of being

Answer *true* or *false* (each answer, 2 points).

11. _____ Singular verbs can sometimes be used with plural nouns.
12. _____ Participles cannot be main verbs without helping verbs.
13. _____ Time is shown by present, past, and future verb tenses.
14. _____ Aesop was known for his parables.
15. _____ A lesson taught in a fable is called a moral.
16. _____ Parables contain the literary elements of good stories, whereas fables do not.
17. _____ Jesus told parables that taught people about God.
18. _____ Setting, plot, and characters are some literary elements of good stories.
19. _____ Events in a fable are true.
20. _____ Morals describe a person's character and conduct and tell how a person can choose between right and wrong.

Draw one line under the verb if the verb is an action verb and draw two lines if the verb shows state of being (each answer, 4 points).
21. A multitude of people crowded around Jesus.
22. A large boulder tumbled off a cliff.
23. The sidewalk is hot.
24. God is the Creator of the universe.
25. Two white sharks suddenly appeared.

Write the word *regular* and *irregular* before each verb (each answer, 1 point).

26._____	redeemed	31._____	caught
27._____	combed	32._____	wrote
28._____	spoke	33._____	cleaned
29._____	sold	34._____	was
30._____	created	35._____	closed

Underline the adverb and circle the word it modifies (each numbered answer, 4 points).

36.   The little boy willingly offered his help.

37.   The old chest plunged quickly to the bottom of the lake.

38.   The package will arrive later.

39.   He did a fairly good job for the first time.

40.   John runs faster than Jason.

Choose the correct word form and write it on the line (each answer, 2 points).

41.   This dough rises (quicker, quick) than the other brand. _____

42.   The couple is (happily, happy) married. _____

43.   Seven of the fish (is, are) lost. _____

44.   The church bell rang (loud, loudly). _____

45.   The money (isn't, aren't) where I put it. _____

Date _____

Score _____

Possible Score _____ 100 _____

113

Name _____

Write *true* or *false* (each answer, 2 points).

1. _____ Literature is the writing of a nation that lasts because of its strength or beauty.
2. _____ Poetry always has rhythm and rhyme.
3. _____ The time covered by a short story is usually the lifetime of the main character.
4. _____ A novel is descriptive, covers a long period of time, and has many characters.
5. _____ A newspaper reports mostly opinions.
6. _____ History is the facts about what countries, people, and nations did over a period of time.
7. _____ A biography is the life history of one person.
8. _____ Fiction is based completely on facts or develops thought or opinion.
9. _____ Drama is written to be acted in front of an audience.
10. _____ A short story involves many characters.

Write the correct letter and answer on each line (each answer, 2 points).

11. A drawing showing how to build a canoe is called a_____ .
    a. diagram   b. chart   c. caption

12. A good reader_____ .
    a.   always reads fast
    b.   only skims for basic information
    c.   fits his speed to his need

13. To find the date of a President's inauguration, a good reader would
    _____ .
    a.   skim the reading material
    b.   outline the reading material
    c.   read the material slowly

14. A caption is_____ .
    a.   a written report
    b.   the words explaining a drawing
    c.   a diagram

15. To find if an article tells about stars, a good reader would_____
    _____ .
    a.   read the article slowly
    b.   skim the article
    c.   scan the article

16. To organize facts about locomotives, a good reader would_____
_____ .
    a. scan the information
    b. write a report
    c. outline

17. A drawing showing the location of a treasure on an island is called___
_____ .
    a. an illustration   b. a chart   c. a map

18. To remember facts for a quiz, a good reader_____ .
    a. scans
    b. reads slowly for details
    c. skims

19. A list of food and their vitamin content is called_____ .
    a. an illustration   b. a chart   c. a map

20. A drawing showing clothes of the eighteenth century is_____
_____ .
    a. a chart   b. an illustration   c. a diagram

Complete these items (each answer, 3 points).

21. A drawing showing how to assemble a model airplane is_____ .

22. For the details of a difficult recipe, a good reader should_____ .
_____ .

23. Something that can be proven is called_____ .

24. Graphic aids include
    a.   _____
    b.   _____
    c.   _____
    d.   _____

Scan the following story and circle the general content of the story (this answer, 2 points).

25.   a wagon train adventure   buffalo life   fire safety

Skim the following story and write the correct answer to each question (each answer, 3 points).

26.   How many wagons were in the train?_____

27.   What type of animal did they see?_____

　　　　We had been on the trail for about a month. The ten wagons in our train traveled slowly across the prairie. I enjoyed seeing the prairie grass blow gently in the breeze. It was a pleasant distraction from the hardships of the trip.

　　　　At one point in our trip, we came upon a small herd of buffalo. Some of our men pursued them for fresh meat. A band of Indians suddenly appeared also hunting the buffalo. Although they seemed friendly, our men decided to hunt later.

　　　　These sights along the trail were interesting but nothing compared to the prairie fire. We saw the smoke in the distance and quickly realized we could not outrun it. We circled the wagons. We got shovels to dig trenches around the wagons. Others manned water buckets in case the fire jumped the trenches. Exhausted we waited for the fire to reach us. We could feel the heat pouring in like waves of water. A yell—a cheer—the wagon train rejoiced together. The trenches worked! This fire was one I would never forget.

Read the story slowly for details and write the correct letter and answer on each line (each answer, 2 points).

28.   They had been on the trail for about_____ .
       a. six weeks   b. ten days   c. a month

29.   The story teller enjoyed seeing_____
       _____ .
       a.   friends along the way
       b.   the prairie grass blow gently in the breeze
       c.   the tall pine trees

30.   A band of Indians_____ .
       a.   were hunting buffalo
       b.   appeared angry at the wagon train
       c.   attacked the wagon train

31.   At first sight of fire, the wagon train_____
       _____ .
       a.   circled and dug trenches
       b.   ran from the fire
       c.   drove around the fire

32.   The fire_____.
        a.   burned several wagons
        b.   reached the wagon train
        c.   burned around the wagon train

Complete the following outline on the story about a wagon train by selecting topics and subtopics from the list; capitalize correctly (each answer, 3 points).

                        Saw smoke in the distance
                        Band of Indians
                        Kept wagons safe
                        The prairie fire
                        Herd of buffalo
                        Circled the wagons

        I.   Sights on the Trail
              A.   Prairie grass
33.   B.   _____
34.   C.   _____
35.   II.   _____
36.   A.   _____
37.   B.   _____
              C.   Dug trenches and readied water
38.   D.   _____

Write *F* if the statement is a fact and *O* if it is an opinion (each answer, 2 points).
39.   _____   I like bacon better than sausage.
40.   _____   Mr. Robert's dog is well trained.
41.   _____   The Pacific Ocean is on the west coast of the United States.

Write a fact and opinion about your home (each answer, 3 points).
42.   fact: _____
43.   opinion: _____

Date _____
Score _____
Possible Score _____ 100 _____

117

Language Arts 510 Alternate Test

Name _____

Match these items (each answer, 2 points).

1. _____ help you visualize places, show size, display information, and so forth
2. _____ decide if people have qualities to be admired or not
3. _____ a word spelled like another word but differing in sound and meaning
4. _____ "Buzz, buzz," said the bee.
5. _____ a phrase or expression whose meaning cannot be understood from the ordinary meanings of the words
6. _____ depends on kinds of words used, action of the story, and suspense
7. _____ asked to see if you understand what you read
8. _____ an outline can be helpful in doing this skill
9. _____ writing based completely on fact or that develops thoughts and opinions
10. _____ a statement that can be proven

a. judging characters
b. reader's enjoyment
c. imitation of sounds
d. nonfiction
e. fact
f. heteronym
g. writing a summary
h. simile
i. idiom
j. graphic aids
k. comprehension questions

Write *true* or *false* (each answer, 2 points).

11. _____ One question you can ask yourself when judging a story's literary value is, "Was the story told in good, clear language?"
12. _____ Reading skills can help you with your Bible study.
13. _____ All poetry must have rhyme and rhythm.
14. _____ Jesus told parables to teach people about God and heaven.
15. _____ An author's purpose is always to entertain his reader.
16. _____ The main idea tells the plot, characters, and setting.
17. _____ Christian judgment is deciding what is right or wrong according to God's Word.
18. _____ Charts display information in a table or graph so that you get information easily.
19. _____ You should never read slowly.
20. _____ Skimming is a similar skill to scanning.

Write the correct letter and answer on each line (each answer, 2 points).

21. The story, "The Man, the Boy, and the Donkey," which has the moral that you cannot please everyone, is an example of a _____ .
    a. parable   b. short story   c. fable
22. The beat heard when a poem is read aloud may also be called _____ .
    a. stress   b. short story   c. simile

23. Palindromes, conundrums, and limericks are _____.
    a. kinds of humor
    b. examples of personification
    c. types of proverbs
24. Bible poetry is written in _____.
    a. metaphors   b. free verse   c. rhyme
25. The phrase, "a plant dies when you do not water it," is an example of

    _____.
    a. sequence of events
    b. cause and effect
    c. main idea
26. The statement, "I think legends are probably true," is an example of

    _____.
    a. an opinion
    b. a fact
    c. author's authority
27. When you decide what probably happened between two events, you

    _____.
    a. place events in sequence
    b. choose the main idea
    c. speculate or infer
28. A drawing that can describe characters and identify a problem is called

    _____.
    a. a diagram   b. a time line   c. an illustration
29. "Come and get it, " yelled Marilyn.
    "Coming!" replied Peggy.
    These lines are an example of_____.
    a. dialogue   b. monologue   c. personal reaction
30. To tell the likenesses and differences of characters is to_____

    _____.
    a. see the author's purpose
    b. compare and contrast
    c. decide fact and opinion

Write the word or words from each sentence that match the description (each answer, 2 points).

The green mountainside was blooming with flowers.
31. participle_____
32. helping verb_____
33. adjective_____
34. subject part_____
35. predicate part_____

The expensive vase tumbled quickly to the floor and it broke.
36. irregular verb_____
37. pronoun_____
38. regular verb_____
39. adverb_____

The triumphantly happy soldier scarcely saw the cheering crowd.
40.   adverb modifying an adjective_____
41.   negative adverb_____
42.   participle used as an adjective modifier_____

Write the possessive form for each word (each answer, 2 points).
43.   ministers_____
44.   leopard_____

Rewrite this sentence in the proper order (this answer, 3 points).
The cat saw the car coming with the black fur.
45._____ .

Punctuate the dialogue correctly (this answer, 3 points).
46.   _____ Would you wash the windows _____ _____ asked Mother _____
_____ Sure _____ _____ replied Jason _____

Write *CS* if the item is a complete sentence and *N* if it is not a sentence (each
answer, 2 points).
47.   _____ The splinter in his finger.
48.   _____ The snake curled around the tree.
49.   _____ He forgave the man.

Date _____
Score _____
Possible Score _____ **100** _____

ANSWER KEYS

SECTION ONE

1.1 Any order:
   a. reading
   b. listening
   c. speaking
   d. writing
1.2 Any order:
   a. Finding main ideas – helps understand message
   b. Noting important details – sharpens imagination
   c. Arranging information in order - helps remember and recall message
   d. Classifying information – helps organize message
   e. Recognizing facts and opinions – helps make good decisions
   f. Making predictions – sharpens anticipation
   g. Identifying plot, setting, and characters – helps share reading experiences
   h. Recognizing accuracy and truthfulness – sharpens ability to make judgments
   i. Developing a vocabulary – increases communication
   j. Developing a good attitude – promotes growth in body, mind, and soul
1.3 a. fat
   b. long
1.4 a. chores
   b. mother and father
   c. chore
   d. chore
   e. chores
   f. chores
   g. chores
   h. you
1.5 chores
1.6 chores
1.7 Example:
   Growing Up With Chores (Topic word should be in the title.)
1.8 nutrition
1.9 Example:
   The Importance of Good Nutrition (Topic word should be in the title.)
1.10 games
1.11 Example:
   Games Are More Than Just Fun (Topic word should be in the title.)
1.12 planets
1.13 Example:
   Our Solar System's Planets (Topic word should be in the title.)
1.14 the Lord
1.15 Example:
   The Lord Will Take Care of Me (Topic word should be in the title.)
1.16 Teacher check
1.17 a. style
   b. topic
1.18 noun
1.19 dialogue
1.20 Quotation
1.21 a. Underline
   b. List
   c. Write
1.22 oil, toy, cow, ouch
1.23 ouch
1.24 cow
1.25 oil
1.26 toy
1.27 one
1.28 proudly; ou; proud; ly; proudly
1.29 abound; ou; a; bound; abound
1.30 account; ou; ac; count; account
1.31 flounder; ou; floun; der; flounder
1.32 vowel; ow; vow; el; vowel

SECTION ONE (cont.)

1.33 tower; ow; tow; er; tower
1.34 powder; ow; pow; der; powder
1.35 prowler; ow; prow; ler; prowler
1.36 jointly; oi; joint; ly; jointly
1.37 doily; oi; doi; ly; doily
1.38 pointing; oi; point; ing; pointing
1.39 boiling; oi; boil; ing; boiling
1.40 voyage; oy; voy; age; voyage
1.41 decoy; oy; de; coy; decoy
1.42 boycott; oy; boy; cott; boycott
1.43 joyous; oy; joy; ous; joyous
1.44 a. 17
     b. 3
1.45 a. fountain
     b. loudly
     c. confound
     d. amount
     e. bounder
     a. Howard
     b. towel
     c. flower
     d. chowder
     e. fowler
1.46 a. Titles will vary.
     b. – k. Answers may vary.

     b. royal
     c. voyage
     d. doily
     e. jointly
     f. boycott
     g. poison
     h. joyous
     i. boiling
     j. pointing
     k. decoy
1.47 In order:
     a. Look at the word and pronounce it.
     b. Listen for all the sounds and spell the word out loud.
     c. Copy the word on paper and read each letter.
     d. Write the word without looking at it. Then check spelling and correct.
     e. Practice writing the word in sentences.
1.48 vowel diphthong
1.49 vowel diphthong
1.50 one
1.51 Any order;
     ou; ow; oi; oy

SECTION TWO

2.1 dialogue or conversation
2.2 The students were on a tour to the Holy Land.
2.3 The students went to the city of Nazareth.
2.4 Either order:
     in the present time
     A.D. 13 (Jesus' day)
2.5 Any order:
     tourists or students or boys and girls
     Dr. Martin
     Jesus
2.6 Example:

Dr. Martin has studied and taught the Bible. He directs tours to the Holy Land. He is an authority.
2.7 Example:
Jesus obeyed His parents and God. He attended school and learned to read.
2.8 The Bible says that Jesus read in the Temple
2.9 Example:
Jesus will help students in all areas of their lives. Jesus is our example.
2.10 wisdom

SECTION TWO (cont.)

2.11 synagogue

2.12 a. Flying to New York
 b. Flying over the Mediterranean Sea
 c. Going to Nazareth on donkeys
 d. Dr. Martin begins talking about Jesus
 e. Students asking questions

2.13 c

2.14 e

2.15 h

2.16 q

2.17 m

2.18 n

2.19 r

2.20 p

2.21 a

2.22 l

2.23 o

2.24 k

2.25 j

2.26 g

2.27 b

2.28 i

2.29 f

2.30 d

2.31 direction

2.32 physical

2.33 account

2.34 tour

2.35 admire

2.36 synagogue

2.37 Nazareth

2.38 ambitious

2.39 Saviour

2.40 memorize

2.41 Mediterranean

2.42 Galilee

2.43 apparently

2.44 approximately

2.45 historian

2.46 diligent

2.47 Anno Domini

2.48 behave

2.49 The entry word shows the correct spelling. The respelling is spelled to show the correct sound — to help pronounce the word.

2.50 Any order:
 a. how many syllables a word has
 b. how vowels are pronounced by use of diacritical marks
 c. where the accent mark is placed

2.51 Across
 1. approximately
 2. ambitious
 3. memorized
 4. admirer
 5. historians
 6. apparently
 7. diligent
 8. synagogue
 9. direction
 10. behave
 Down
 1. physical
 2. Anno Domini
 3. Mediterranean
 4. accounts
 5. tour
 6 Saviour
 7. Galilee
 8. Nazareth

2.52 eastern; ea; east; ern; eastern

2.53 crooked; oo; crook; ed; crooked

2.54 toothache; oo; tooth; ache; toothache

2.55 fewer; ew; few; er; fewer

2.56 freedom; ee; free; dom; freedom

2.57 failure; ai; fail; ure; failure

SECTION TWO (cont.)

2.58 praying; ay; pray; ing; praying

2.59 roaster; oa; roast; er; roaster

2.60 growing; ow; grow; ing; growing

2.61 saucer; au; sau; cer; saucer

2.62 Teacher check

2.63 vowel digraph

2.64 one

2.65 Any four; any order

2.66 verb

2.67 adjective

2.68 adverb

SECTION THREE

3.1 Either order:
a. reading
b. writing

3.2 leaders of the Temple who were very educated

3.3 wrote a message in the sand

3.4 a. skills
b. communicate

3.5 thoughtful

3.6 careless or forgetful

3.7 a. hand
b. do
c. might

3.8 a. approve or confirm
b. hands

3.9 Any order:
a. space
b. shape
c. size
d. stroke
e. slant

3.10 Teacher check

3.11 Teacher check

3.12 Teacher check

3.13 Teacher check

3.14 advise

3.15 achieve

3.16 active

3.17 arrange

3.18 believe

3.19	climate		3.28	obscure
3.20	college		3.29	peaceful
3.21	elate		3.30	secure
3.22	expense		3.31	suppose
3.23	figure		3.32	treasure
3.24	forehead		3.33	Tuesday
3.25	homestead		3.34	(see below)
3.26	minute			
3.27	mistake			

3.34

```
A C R W Z M N L O G B R O L S L O R M N Z V X
U N U T M O Z B I R E T A L E F G H I T Z E W
R B Y G H T O E P T I O H A P U P I S I A V N
G R N E N A M V N A R A K M A C E A J U T H O
S O Z L M N O B R T U V L S R D A I A D K N L
I O M R T E H R D Y D A D B A R C O H R E S C
F G I V N O W R S E N O V U T U E S D A Y M O
O P U T A R R A N G E Z L Z E P F V O J K T R
B O J K D B D F H J L N P Q O S U B E R O L B
S E M I V L O K C N I E H T M E L S L E S H A
C H L E I N U Y O S K E R M N O N W I O L M L
U A R I S E A V L O U S E S U P P O S E R V C
R W X L E U V M N Z P R S Q R V L O P T M U K
E H C A R V A C T I V E N I H E T S Q U I E T
L X T R Y O E W L I G W R O W L I D N N I O
E I P T M E G E R I T O E P E L G V E I A W J
V A Y E T G I T F O M V E O D G O H D M A S Y
A O T G N V E R V E N A H W L I S B R I C T E
E D A Y C S L W W T P I T G F O R E H E A D G
M Y F H O M E S T E A D Y E N S F T C M W H A
I Y N S L F A O R P Y L I G H A W W H U H W N
S G Y P L I A T E O F T I T W H T G T H R M R
A C H I E V E Y A N A B H G W T T T Y N L E O
B H A Y G W B U S H E L N B W A F I Y L K H C
R O E H E H P T U N L O F S Y T M U M A E H I
L W A B F I G U R E O Y S E W Y F A T T D A X
V H W H D I T S E C T I S V B I H S I S N B M
M F T S W W T P I O L G B T W A I M A B O P U
N P G M K N W S R O T C S I V M B L O G H N V
```

SECTION ONE

0.1 Teacher check

1.1 Armstrong Sperry

1.2 He spent two years exploring the South Pacific. His great-grandfather had told him about thrilling adventures in the South Seas.

1.3 He received the Newberry Award.

1.4 Mafatu lived on the island of Hikueru in the South Pacific.

1.5 Tavana Nui was the village chief and Mafatu's father.

1.6 Mafatu was afraid of the sea.

1.7 Mafatu was with his mother during the hurricane.

1.8 Mafatu thought about the sea when he heard it at night and when he tried to fish.

1.9 Everyone rejected Mafatu because he was afraid.

1.10 Uri was a skinny yellow dog, and Kivi was a crippled albatross.

1.11 Kana called Mafatu a coward, and he was Mafatu's best friend.

1.12 Moana was the sea god whom Mafatu learned to believe was going to get him.

1.13 Mafatu left his home the night before all the village boys were going on a bonito hunt.

1.14 Example:
Mafatu may have taken Kana's boat, so Kana would know he was not a coward.

1.15 Example:
Tavana Nui's silence shamed Mafatu because, as his son, he was supposed to be brave. The other boys' fathers would be talking about their sons.

1.16 Mafatu chose Uri and Kivi because they were rejected also.

1.17 c

1.18 f

1.19 i

1.20 e

1.21 g

1.22 a

1.23 h

1.24 d

1.25 j

1.26 k

1.27 Ball C

action	-	behavior
group	-	classify
make	-	develop
ability	-	intelligence
trust	-	faith
know	-	identify
arrange	-	organize
notice	-	recognize
effort	-	challenge
match	-	compare
talk	-	discussion
learn	-	remember

1.28-1.32 Examples:

1.28 a. Pacific Islands in the Pacific Ocean
b. Year-round temperature 77 degrees, rainy

1.29 Either order:
a. Tall, well-shaped bodies
b. Light skin, dark hair

1.30 Either order:
   a. Before Christianity, ancestor worship
   b. Worshiped power
1.31 a. Wood frame homes, thatched roofs
   b. Cotton waistcloth called Pareu
1.32 Any order:
   a. Skillful seafarers (fishermen)
   b. Skilled craftsmen
   c. Some fruit farmers
1.33 F
1.34 O
1.35 F
1.36 F
1.37 O
1.38 O
1.39 O
1.40 F
1.41 F
1.42 O
1.43-1.47 Any order within column:

headache	ghost-spirit	tidal wave
1.43 outrigger	barrier-reef	sea urchin
1.44 someone	tiger-shark	village house
1.45 sunset	long-drawn	Sea God
1.46 fishermen	high-held	
1.47 millrace		

1.48 Any order:
   someone, sailboat, icehouse, barefoot, houseboat, ice cream, blacksmith, chalkboard, schoolhouse, birdhouse, iceboat, schoolyard, grandmother, stepmother, blackberry
1.49 a. whosoever
   b. the student's name
1.50 a. chal/lenge   11
   b. clas/sify   ss
   c. discus/sion   ss
   d. intel/ligent   11

1.51 Either order:
   a. 11
   b. ss
1.52 double consonants or consonant twins
1.53 a. 2
   b. 1
   c. 2
   d 3
   e. 2
   f. 3
   g. 3
   h. 2
   i. 2
   j. 1
   k. 3
1.54 no
1.55 yes
1.56 syllables
1.57 a. 3   b. after noon
1.58 a. 2   b. brand new
1.59 a. 2   b. child hood
1.60 a. 2   b. deer skin
1.61 a. 4   b. evil doer
1.62 a. 3   b. fisher man
1.63 a. 2   b. grape fruit
1.64 a. 2   b. hard ship
1.65 a. 2   b. in let
1.66 a. 2   b. jay bird
1.67 a. 2   b. key board
1.68 a. 2   b. land scape
1.69 a. 2   b. moon light
1.70 friend check
1.71 Check with example.
1.72 Check with example.
1.73 Check with example.
1.74 Check with example.

SECTION TWO

2.1	Kana
2.2	boy
2.3	albatross
2.4	lagoon
2.5	Mafatu
2.6	canoe
2.7	bonitos
2.8	albatross
2.9	palms
2.10	people
2.11	Choices will vary.
2.12	Choices will vary.
2.13	Choices will vary.
2.14	nouns
2.15	Risk-taking is necessary to grow into mature, useful adults. *or* Courage is developed when a person decides to take a risk.
2.16	risk-taking
2.17	Risk-Taking Helps Us Grow
2.18	Check LIFEPAC, page 27.
2.19	A nondescript yellow dog named Uri.
2.20	He had a thin coat and puzzled and true eyes.
2.21	Uri followed the boy wherever he went.
2.22	on his lonely wanderings
2.23	older birds
2.24	Something about the bird's trying to fight off its more powerful fellows touched his heart.
2.25	in the shallow of the lagoon

2.26	when it learned to fly
2.27	Mafatu was envious of Kivi's freedom and ability to get away.
2.28	Mafatu's friends were Uri and Kivi.
2.29	yellow dog
2.30	thin coat
2.31	puzzled eyes
2.32	lonely wanderings
2.33	powerful fellows
2.34	effortless flight
2.35	envious eyes
2.36	among
2.37	business
2.38	believe
2.39	busy
2.40	doctor
2.41	forty
2.42	laid
2.43	minute
2.44	minute
2.45	raise
2.46	separate
2.47	a. among
	b. believe
	c. busy
	d. business
	e. doctor
	f. minute
	g. forty
	h. separate
	i. laid
	j. raise

2.48 Any ordered

a. among
b. business
c. busy
d. doctor
e. forty
f. laid
g. minute
h. believe
i. raise
j. separate

```
B V O L D B M O S A
M U A M O N G B E Z
I D S F C G L U P B
N O O I T L F S A U
U W I F O R T Y R S
T N H U R A C D A I
E L R A I S E O T N
L A I D O S R I E E
B E L I E V E W M S
A X C Y D W E V B S
```

2.49 c
2.50 o
2.51 u
2.52 r
2.53 a
2.54 g

2.55 e
2.56 courage
2.57 God promises to reward our work.
2.58 The book of the law, God's Word, the Bible, must be read.
2.59 Yes, it is very hard to obey God and not do what we want to do.
2.60 God promises success, prosperity, and that He will be with you wherever you go.
2.61 yes
2.62 Examples; any order:
1. Reward my works
2. Make my way prosperous
3. Give me success
4. Be with me wherever I go
2.63 Teacher check

SECTION THREE

3.1   Examples:

    a. terror, anxiety

    b. anxiety, sadness

    c. shame, resentment

    d. shame, disappointment

    e. pride, happiness

    f. anger, embarrassment

    g. sympathy, joy

    h. anxiety, nervousness

3.2   anxious - (uneasy)

    disgusting - (repulsive)

    embarrass - (shame)

    envious - (jealous)

    enthusiasm - (zeal)

    resentment - (offense)

    sympathy - (pity

    violence - (fury)

3.3   Noun

3.4   Adjective

3.5   Verb

3.6   Noun

3.7   Verb

3.8   Adjective

3.9   Noun

3.10   line five

3.11   Poems will vary, but must follow the diamante pattern. They must also display a change of mood, or attitude, from line one to line seven, the change to occur in line five.

3.12   a. will not

    b. is not

    c. have not

    d. would not

    e. cannot

    f. shall not

    g. she will

    h. you have

    i. should have

    j. let us

    k. we will

    l. should not

    m. they are

    n. he is

    o. she is

    p. it is

    q. we would

    r. you are

    s. I have

    t. we have

    u. they would

    v. do not

    w. could have

    x. would have

3.13   a. isn't

    b. haven't

    c. wouldn't

    d. shan't

    e. can't

    f. won't

    g. He's

    h. She's

    i. It's

SECTION ONE

1.1 a. true
     b. false
     c. true
     d. true
     e. true
     f. true
     g. false
     h. false
     i. true
     j. true

1.2 a. Gardening is a favorite pastime.

1.3 a. God and man have been gardening since man was created.

1.4 a. God talked to man in the garden.

1.5 c. Adam noticed that no animal looked like a man.

1.6 b. Language started with the first man.

1.7 a. 3
     b. 1
     c. 4
     d. 2
     e. 5
     f. 6

1.8 Example:
God talked to man in the garden of Eden. God told Adam to name all the animals. The Bible tells us.

1.9 a. rek′ urd
     b. ri kôrd′
     c. min′ it
     d. mī nüt′
     e. bō

     f. bou
     g. wīnd
     h. wind
     i. red
     j. rēd

1.10 Down:
     1. characteristics
     6. theory
     Across:
     2. authentic
     3. evolved
     4. scholar
     5. intelligent
     7. curious
     Secret Message: God loves you.

1.11 d
1.12 g
1.13 a
1.14 j
1.15 f
1.16 l
1.17 b
1.18 h
1.19 c
1.20 i
1.21 e
1.22 k
1.23 a. s
      b. s
      d. s
      f. s
      h. s

SECTION ONE (cont.)

1.24 a. Missionaries in jungle territories work with native tribes.

     b. God can talk.

     c. John and his father played a game.

     d. John planned to win the race.

     e. Mother watched the children play.

1.25 Teacher check

1.26 Teacher check

1.27 a. au
     b. ai
     c. ay
     d. ee
     e. ai
     f. oo
     g. au
     h. ew
     i. ea
     j. ai
     k. ea
     l. oo
     m. ew
     n. ai
     o. ee
     p. au
     q. oo
     r. ea
     s. ea
     t. oo

1.28 Any order:
     a. automatic
       inauguration
       somersault
     b. betrayal
     c. available
       faithfully
       maintenance
       remainder
     d. neighborhood
       woodpecker
     e. jewelry
       newscaster
     f. exceedingly
       seventeenth
     g. leadership
       meaningful
       underneath
       uneasy
     h. foolishness
       soothingly

1.29 a. 4
     b. 4
     c. 5
     d. 3
     e. 3
     f. 3

SECTION TWO

2.1 a. Johnny was anxious to get to school on time. He rode his bicycle through his neighbor's flower garden.

b. "Johnny": screamed the angry neighbor, "You are destroying the beautiful flowers!"

c. Lucifer decided to become greater than Jehovah God. God cast him out of heaven.

d. The children in the neighborhood teased Mickey every day. Mickey ran home crying.

2.2 a. 3   e. 2
b. 4   f. 4
c. 2   g. 3
d. 1   h. 1

2.3-2.5 Examples:

2.3 Adam and Eve disobeyed God. Their disobedience made them sinners, and their sin changed them.

2.4 The two sons of Adam and Eve brought sacrifices to God. Abel's offering was pleasing to God. Cain's offering was unacceptable to God.

2.5 Cain's jealousy of his brother led Cain to misuse language. Cain killed his brother.

2.6

	Prefix	Suffix	Root Word
a.		x	German
b.		x	approximate
c.		x	translate
d.		x	fact
e.	x	x	event
f.	x	x	appreciate
g.		x	nomad
h.	x	x	intelligent
i.	x	x	obey
j.	x		patient
k.	x		advantage
l.	x		accurate
m.	x		interpret

2.7 a. un
b. in
c. im
d. in
e. in
f. un
g. im
h. im
i. un
j. un

2.8 bicycle
2.9 antisocial
2.10 displease
2.11 nonfiction
2.12 prearrange
2.13 pro-American
2.14 replace
2.15 supernatural
2.16 mislead

SECTION TWO (cont.)

2.17 a. able
b. ful
c. less
d. ful
e. able
f. able
g. ful
h. less
i. ful
j. less

2.18 a. pleasant
b. kindly

2.19 sweeten

2.20 writer

2.21 laughed

2.22 allowance

2.23 painless

2.24 Singing

2.25 use wrongly; make wrong use of

2.26 admitting one's sins

2.27 failure to obey

2.28 a good chance; favorable time

2.29 that which is offered to God

2.30 person having much knowledge

2.31 sly; tricky

2.32 not worth taking

2.33-2.37 Examples:

2.33 The little bird learned to eat flower seeds.

2.34 Strong boys can run a mile.

2.35 Early people learned to farm the land.

2.36 Astronauts can fly to the moon.

2.37 The friendly dog found the lost boys.

2.38 a. A, beautiful, the
b. The, thoughtful, our
c. The, fussy, their
d. a, sparkling, the
e. The, serious

2.39 a. prosperous
b. moonlit
c. unbearable
d. memorable
e. adventurous
f. enormous

2.40 a. well
b. often
c. loudly
d. slowly
e. smoothly
f. very

2.41 Examples:
a. Wash your hands often.
b. Answer very quickly when you are called.
c. Did you do your work well?
d. Look both ways carefully before crossing a street.
e. Tell others boldly that you love Jesus.

2.42 Teacher check

2.43 Teacher check

2.44 Teacher check

2.45 a. bristle
b. kneel
c. knight
d. wrist
e. chalk
f. hasten
g. knowledge
h. wrestle
i. daughter
j. glisten
k. wrench
l. fasten
m. freight
n. knot
o. wreckage
p. salmon
q. folks
r. sigh
s. flight
t. stalk

2.46 Any order:
a. silent "t"
   bristle
   hasten
   wrestle
   glisten
   fasten
b. silent "k"
   kneel
   knight
   knot
   knowledge
c. silent "w"
   wrench
   wreckage
   wrestle
   wrist
d. silent "l"
   chalk
   folks
   salmon
   stalk
e. silent "gh"
   knight
   daughter
   freight
   sigh
   flight

2.47 a. wreckage
     b. salmon
     c. glisten
     d. knight
     e. wrestle
2.48 Examples:
     a. A brush with stiff bristles is good for cleaning your teeth.
     b. Fasten your seatbelt before you begin your trip.
     c. The water in the pond will glisten in the sunlight.
     d. She will hasten to complete her spelling assignment.
     e. I do not have enough knowledge about that subject.
     f. Her long sigh made me realize that she was discouraged.
     g. Corn grows on a stalk.
     h. When we saw the wreckage of the accident, we were reminded to drive carefully.
     i. The handle broke when she gave it a sudden wrench.
     j. She has a gold bracelet on her left wrist.

SECTION THREE

3.1 <u>to inform</u>

3.2 <u>to entertain</u>

3.3 to give directions

3.4 to entertain

3.5 Examples:
to give men directions, inform
us of His plan of salvation,
to guide men

3.6 a. Therefore they thank our Lord
Jesus Christ, of whom
proceedeth all wisdom and
all goodness.
b. Wherefore I beseech you
meekly for the mercy of God,
that ye pray for me that Christ
have mercy on me and forgive
my guilt.

3.7 Examples:
blast-off, astronaut, NASA,
splashdown, burnup, module,
moonlanding

3.8 a. people
b. events
c. inventions

3.9 false

3.10 true

3.11 true

3.12 false

3.13 true

3.14 true

3.15 the Flood

3.16 The church began.

3.17 eternity

3.18 In order:
Anglo-Saxons settle in England.
Normans conquer Anglo-Saxons.
Pilgrims come to America.
Indian words are added.
Other Europeans add words.

3.19 alter

3.20 bawl

3.21 creak

3.22 flee

3.23 fir

3.24 heal
he'll

3.25 hoarse

3.26 minor

3.27 wring

3.28 pause

3.29 site
cite

3.30 to drill a hole or make tired
male pig or hog

3.31 an army officer
a seed of corn

3.32 what is being carried
vein of metal ore

3.33 loud noise
light bat for hitting tennis balls

3.34 writing or letter-paper
not moving

3.35 c

3.36 e

3.37 g

3.38 h

3.39 d

3.40 a

3.41 j

3.42 i

3.43 b

3.44 f

3.45 Teacher check

3.46 a. Street or Saint
b. Avenue
c. Monday
d. Tuesday
e. Wednesday
f. Thursday
g. Friday
h. Saturday
i. Sunday
j. January
k. February

l.   March
m. April
n.   August
o.   September
p.   October
q.   November
r.   December
s.   Genesis or General
t.   Revelation or Reverend
u.   Deuteronomy
v.   Psalms or Psalm
w. Proverbs
x.   Matthew
y.   Ephesians
z.   Leviticus
aa. Colossians or Colonel

3.47   a.   cup
b.   large
c.   teaspoon
d.   dozen
e.   minute
f.   tablespoon
g.   teaspoons

3.48   a.   leave
b.   arrive

3.49   a.   North
b.   South
c.   East
d.   West

3.50   a.   kilowatt
b.   kilogram
c.   kilometer
d.   centimeter
e.   decimeter
f.   millimeter

3.51   environment
3.52   Germanic
3.53   squire
3.54   monk
3.55   entangle
3.56   revenge
3.57   abound
3.58   gourmet
3.59   scop

3.60   cobbler
3.61   nomadic
3.62   Teacher check
3.63   Teacher check
3.64   Teacher check
3.65   Teacher check
3.66   g
3.67   j
3.68   a
3.69   b
3.70   i
3.71   c
3.72   f
3.73   h
3.74   e
3.75   d
3.76   advance (or retreat)
       retreat (or advance)
3.77   gush
       trickle
3.78   attract
       repel
3.79   sorrowful
       joyous
3.80   formal
       casual
3.81   preserve
       destroy
3.82   compliment
       insult
3.83   Either order:
       fiction
       fact
3.84   Either order:
       deny
       admit
3.85   a.   encourage
       b.   discourage

SECTION ONE

1.1	a	1.29	F
1.2	Eating snow and licking icicles can be dangerous to your health.	1.30	O
		1.31	F
1.3	g	1.32	O
1.4	n	1.33	F
1.5	d	1.34	O
1.6	j	1.35	question (?)
1.7	a	1.36	statement (.)
1.8	m	1.37	statement (.)
1.9	b	1.38	request-command (.)
1.10	c	1.39	exclamation (!)
1.11	e	1.40	question (?)
1.12	f	1.41	command (.)
1.13	l	1.42	statement (.)
1.14	h	1.43	question (?)
1.15	i	1.44	exclamation (!) or statement (.)

1.16 Dr. George Meyer, an environmental geologist, and Dr. David Grandstaff, a geochemist, analyzed what was in the snow.

1.17 The snow collects particles of industrial wastes and automobile exhaust fumes.

1.18 Snowfall in rural areas contains lead content.

1.19 A small percentage of pollution comes from industrial waste. Ninety percent or more can be traced to automobile gasoline, released through exhaust fumes.

1.20 A small percentage of the pollution in snow comes from industrial waste, particularly from paint factories.

1.21 The report said that snow was heavily laced with lead, an accumulative poison. The lead is trapped while snow is falling.

1.22 no support

1.23 c

1.24 b

1.25 e

1.26 a

1.27 f

1.28 F

1.45 may
1.46 Thank-you
1.47 sorry
1.48 excuse me
1.49 Good morning
1.50 Hello
1.51 a. thank you
    b. please
    c. sorry
    d. excuse me
    e. forgive me
1.52 teacher check
1.53 a. add, d
    b. banner, n
    c. castle, t, e
    d. egg, g
    e. filled, l, e
    f. ghost, h
    g. gnat, g
    h. knife, k, e
    i. listen, t
    j. muscle, c, e
    k. pneumonia, p
    l. scenery, c
1.54-1.65 Teacher check
1.66 Teacher check

SECTION TWO

2.1	Joe and his friend
2.2	Joe
2.3	Bob
2.4	Joe
2.5	Bob
2.6	caught four large fish
2.7	wanted them to clean the fish
2.8	cleaned two fish
2.9	enjoyed a tasty fish supper
2.10	talked about the fun of fishing
2.11	blue
2.12	billowing
2.13	thundering
2.14	brown, grizzly
2.15	sleepy
2.16	anxious
2.17	growling
2.18	purring
2.19	humorous
2.20	tragic
2.21	four
2.22	six
2.23	many
2.24	several
2.25	few
2.26	those
2.27	these
2.28	this
2.29	that
2.30	first
2.31	nouns
2.32	kind
2.33	many
2.34	one
2.35	The, monkey, a, nut, the, head, a, man
2.36	an, egg, the, floor
2.37	The, blue, book, a, sick, child
2.38	quickly; how
2.39	here; where
2.40	late; when

2.41	loudly; how
2.42	neatly; how
2.43	there; where
2.44	soon; when
2.45	loudly; how
2.46	here; where
2.47	there; where
2.48	patiently; how
2.49-2.57	Examples:
2.49	The tired boys <u>slowly</u> found their way home.
2.50	Mother <u>lovingly</u> hugged the lost boys.
2.51	Father spoke <u>kindly</u> to the officer.
2.52	The snow fell <u>everywhere</u>.
2.53	Everyone knew the boys were to be found <u>somewhere</u>.
2.54	The excitement <u>soon</u> calmed down.
2.55	People were <u>now</u> waiting for the news.
2.56	We will go <u>then</u>.
2.57	The choir director said, "<u>Now</u> Sing!"
2.58	Teacher check
2.59	2
2.60	7
2.61	1
2.62	5
2.63	3
2.64	4
2.65	8
2.66	6
2.67	9
2.68	10
2.69	14
2.70	11
2.71	12
2.72	13
2.73	Example:

SECTION TWO (cont.)

Robin Hood was a young man who desired to serve the King. The Chief Forester was a dishonest officer who wanted to appear to have done his duty.

2.74 Example:
The Saxon woodsmen were honest workmen. The foresters were dishonest men who forced people to help perform their evil deeds.

2.75 Example:
Both men wanted to fight for the freedom of others.

2.76 Example:
Will risked his life to free Robin and Robin risked his life to free the captives.

2.77-2.82 Examples:

2.77 false pride

2.78 deceitful

2.79 dishonesty

2.80 cruel

2.81 thoughtless

2.82 thoughtless - self-centered

2.83 unwise

2.84 wise

2.85 wise

2.86 wise

2.87 yes

2.88 Examples:
He may have been captured in another way. He may have asked to join the wicked foresters. He may have had an opportunity to get to Nottingham.

2.89 teacher check

2.90 M

2.91 S

2.92 c

2.93 e

2.94 f

2.95 g

2.96 a

2.97 b

2.98-2.104 Any order:

2.98 cough

2.99 enough

2.100 fantastic

2.101 frequent

2.102 phantom

2.103 physical

2.104 telephone or confident

2.105-2.107 Any order:

2.105 gh

2.106 f

2.107 ph

2.108 Any order:

Any order:	Any order:
a. celebrate	f. cough
b. celery	g. compliment
c. celestial	h. confident
d. citizen	i. cucumber
e. cylinder	

2.109 e, i, y

2.110 o, u

2.111 Teacher check

SECTION THREE

3.1	Teacher check	3.17	a fruit that grows on trees
3.2	Teacher check	3.18	a loud sound
3.3	Teacher check	3.19	outer part or edge of something
3.4	Teacher check	3.20	not moving
3.5	Teacher check	3.21	hair
3.6	h	3.22	pair or pare
3.7	c	3.23	peel
3.8	i	3.24	boarder
3.9	g	3.25	stationery
3.10	j	3.26	a growth from the skin
3.11	b	3.27	a set of two *or* to remove the outer covering or skin
3.12	d	3.28	outer covering of fruit
3.13	f	3.29	person who pays for room and meals
3.14	a	3.30	writing material
3.15	e	3.31	check with example
3.16	long-eared member of the rabbit family		

SECTION ONE

1.1 Examples:
   a. alighted
   b. knights
   c. liege
   d. midst
   e. pulleth
   Others:
   arms
   jousting
   multitude
   men-at-arms
   my pleasure to accord it
   homage
   seneschal
   lodging

1.2 a. wondrously, wondering, wonderful
   b. marvelous
   c. miraculous
   d. fortunate

1.3 carried him away

1.4 circled restlessly

1.5 pulled their mightiest

1.6 Example:
   All the barons and knights of
   Britain came to try to pull a
   sword out of a stone. Young
   Arthur pulled it out easily.
   None of the other knights could.

1.7 b, c, or d

1.8 c

1.9 c

1.10 d or c

1.11 b or c

1.12 Examples:
   a. At the sight of this marvel, the
      crowd's excitement increased.
   b. None could budge the sword by so
      much as a fraction of an inch.
   c. When Arthur laid his hand on the
      jewelled hilt, the sword came free
      from its resting place.

   d. Now let me see whether you can put
      the sword where it was and draw it
      forth again.
   e. The Archbishop counseled them to
      remain quiet till after the trial in
      public.

1.13 d

1.14 a

1.15 f

1.16 c

1.17 b

1.18 Bible

1.19 Bible, social studies

1.20 language arts

1.21 Bible, science, social studies

1.22 social studies, language arts

1.23 Bible

1.24 science, art

1.25 science, Bible, social studies

1.26 mathematics

1.27 social studies, language arts

1.28 social studies

1.29 social studies, Bible, language arts

1.30 social studies, Bible, language arts

1.31 language arts

1.32 Bible

1.33 science, social studies

1.34 language arts

1.35 language arts

1.36 science

1.37 mathematics

1.38 art

1.39 Bible, science

1.40 mathematics, art

1.41 Bible

1.42 Having the nature of a miracle
     wondrous; marvelous.

1.43 Make grow, or keep alive and
     well, with food.

1.44 The king or lord who has the right
     to the homage and loyal service of
     his vassals.

1.45 Weapons; the use of weapons; fighting; war.

1.46 A noisy quarrel.

1.47 A person who follows or succeeds another person in office.

1.48 A group of attendants.

1.49 An iron or steel block on which metals are hammered.

1.50 A great many; crowd.

1.51 Establish as law; fix; decide; appoint.

1.52 Example:
Sir Ector would be sure his son was telling the truth if he swore by the Bible.

1.53 Example:
The knights would believe if they saw proof, but not if they heard about it from Arthur or Sir Ector.

1.54 The knights wrangled over Uther's successor. (Sentence 2)

1.55 The Archbishop called together all of the men-at-arms. (Sentence 1)

1.56 A great marble stone had appeared. (Sentence 1)

1.57 Every man wanted to be the first to try to draw out the sword. (Sentence 3)

1.58 None could budge the sword. (Sentence 3)

1.59 Word of a tournament was sent throughout the land. (Sentence 2)

1.60-1.67 Examples:

1.60 c or a

1.61 d or e

1.62 a or d

1.63 f

1.64 e

1.65 b or a or d

1.66 a or d

1.67 c

1.68 a. good
b. good
c. not good

1.69 a. good
b. good
c. good

1.70 a. not good
b. good
c. not good

1.71 Example:
People told stories about Arthur and perhaps made them more exciting by adding imaginative details. The stories grew more imaginative every time they were told.

1.72 Example:
Sir Ector would not have asked Sir Kay to swear. Possible Bible verses: Matthew 5:34 through 37; James 5:12.

1.73 excitement
Example:
Everyone joined in the excitement of the school picnic.

1.74 amazement
Example:
The boy's eyes grew wide with amazement.

1.75 achievement
Example:
To get a perfect score was a fine achievement.

1.76 employment
Example:
Even boys and girls can find some kind of employment for a few hours.

1.77 advancement
Example:
Hard work is usually rewarded by advancement.

1.78 restless, unable to rest

1.79 helpless, unable to help oneself

SECTION ONE (cont.)

1.80 sleepless, doing without sleep or unable to sleep

1.81 borderless, without a border

1.82 brimless, without a brim

1.83 science
one who works in science

1.84 art
one who works in art

1.85 bicycle
one who rides a bicycle

1.86 girl
one who acts like a girl

1.87 fool
one who acts like a fool

1.88 man
one who acts like a man

1.89 a. art
b. girl
c. fool

1.90 bicycle

1.91 science

1.92 man

1.93 Teacher check

SECTION TWO

2.1 Teacher check

2.2 the first sentence

2.3 the third sentence

2.4 She let us know Roger's thoughts.

2.5 Roger is talking to himself.

2.6 Examples:
It makes Roger more real.
We think we know Roger.

2.7 Example:
She thought Roger would figure out what was the right thing to do with God's help because he had already told God he was sorry.

2.8 Teacher check

2.9 Examples:
a. "It's time to go, dear. Take Mommy's hand and let's go."
b. "I've had enough of this dawdling! Now hurry!"
c. "Dear, it's time to leave. Couldn't you please hurry a little?"
d. "Hoowee up! We dotta do!"
e. "Hurry as quickly as you can, class. It is time to leave."

2.10 "Who called me?" asked Peter.

2.11 "I did," whispered Donald from the bushes.

2.12 Peter looked around and saw Donald. "What are you doing there?" he blurted.

2.13 "Hiding from Al," Donald said quietly.

2.14 Peter laughed and said, "Whatever for?"

2.15 Teacher check

2.16 Sentences may vary:
a. Louellen was standing near her locker at school, talking with friends.
b. Cynthia, a new girl at school, came to her locker near Louellen's.
c. Louellen said, "Hello" to Cynthia.
d. Louellen turned her back on Cynthia.
e. Louellen started talking with her friends again.
f. Louellen thought she probably hadn't been kind to Cynthia.
g. Louellen turned back to Cynthia and drew her into the circle.
h. Louellen introduced Cynthia to the other girls.

2.17 Example:
The boy without a jacket was cold riding his bicycle.

2.18 Example:
Jack could not ride his bicycle
because it had only one wheel.
(or, which had only one wheel)

2.19 Example:
Mike had a cold, but he couldn't
wait to try out his new football.

2.20 Example:
Alice thought it was a good day
to swim because it was sunny.

2.21 Example:
While standing on the corner, I
was scared by an automobile horn.

2.22 Examples:
Did you see a boy with a cowboy
hat in the bus?

2.23 anyway

2.24 besides

2.25 fewer

2.26 accept

2.27 well

2.28 taught

2.29 Let

2.30 materialism

2.31 Americanism

2.32 Catholicism

2.33 Communism

2.34 heroism

2.35 nationalism

2.36 organism

2.37 realism

2.38 witticism

2.39 eighth

2.40 realism (other answers possible)

2.41 twelfth

2.42 hundredth

2.43 organism

2.44 witticisms

2.45 Americanism or nationalism

2.46 materialism

2.47 Teacher check

SECTION THREE

3.1 Example:
Boy gets the job. Dog runs away. Boy's experiences finding dog before the owners come home.

3.2 Example:
Problems and troubles of one boy or girl, or competition between two friends - a close finish or a surprise ending.

3.3 Example:
The time your grandma's cousins talked her into riding a bony old cow and it ran away with her.

3.4 Example:
You could be the youngest person ever to make a parachute jump

3.5 I. Hint:
The setting should be simple and a place the writer knows.
II. Hint:
The characters should be the kinds of people the writer knows. No more than three or four characters should be in the story.
III. Hint:
One central problem or challenge is better than several in a short story.

3.6 Hint:
The writer should tell more about the character than just his or her physical characteristics.

3.7 Teacher check

3.8 don't

3.9 thought

3.10 wasn't

3.11 Examples:
lovely pale green; blue lace

3.12 Examples:
exciting; close-called

3.13 Examples:
hard working; overworked

3.14 Example:
Bob ran like a deer to tag the runner.

3.15 Example:
Jane dawdled as she walked down the street. or Jane dragged her feet.

3.16 Alex is a whiz on the basketball court. or Alex plays basketball with skill.

3.17 Example:
Mother's dinner was out of this world.

3.18 Anyway, I didn't want to go with the other boys.

3.19 Are there any cookies other than the stale ones?

3.20 My older brother taught me to ice skate.

3.21 "Why couldn't I have gone!" exclaimed Joe.

3.22 "Why couldn't I go?" asked Joe.

3.23 Joe said with pleasure, "It's an excellent day for fishing."

3.24 "Hooray! It's a holiday!" exclaimed Betsy

3.25 "Come along," said Mr. Jones.

3.26 "Do you think we can find any treasure in the old mine?" whispered Pete.

3.27 Teacher check

3.28 Teacher check

3.29 not guarded; no one keeping watch

3.30 not wanted

3.31 not fair

3.32 used against enemy aircraft

3.33 used against disease-causing bacteria

3.34 something formed by living organisms to fight disease

3.35 the last great enemy of Christ

3.36 a liquid with a low freezing point

3.37 opposed to trusts

3.38 opposed to friendly relationships with others

3.39 a medicine that counteracts the effects of poison

3.40 a substance that prevents the growth of germs

3.41 Teacher check

SECTION ONE

1.1   e

1.2   f

1.3   c

1.4   b

1.5   a

1.6   c

1.7   b

1.8   a

1.9   b

1.10   c

1.11   Example:
The conqueror comes with roll of stirring drums and the trumpet that sings of fame. The Pilgrims came with true hearts and with hymns of lofty cheer.

1.12   Examples:
a. fearless, truthful, having deep love
b. serene, confident, calm
c. eager

1.13   Example:
Other people often seek jewels, wealth, or the spoils of war. The pilgrims sought a place to worship in freedom according to their faith.

1.14   Any order:
a. meadows rich with corn
b. cool September morn
c. orchards with ripe apples and peaches
d. pleasant morn of the early fall

1.15   Any order:
a. Frederick was green-walled by the hills of Maryland.
b. Round about them orchards sweep.
c. Lee marched over the mountain wall.
d. Over the mountains, winding down into town.

1.16   in the morning

1.17   noon

1.18   Union

1.19   They were afraid of what the Confederates would do.

1.20   "To show that one heart was loyal yet."

1.21   banner, silken scarf, free flag, torn folds, flag of freedom and union, symbol of light and law, thy stars

1.22   The rebel rides no more. Barbara Frietchie is dead. Stonewall Jackson is dead.

1.23   Freedom to worship according to the Pilgrims' faith is pictured in the first poem. Freedom to be loyal to one's country is pictured in the second poem.

1.24   false

1.25   true

1.26   true

1.27   false

1.28   false

1.29   true

1.30   C

1.31   RR

1.32   RR

1.33   C

1.34   Teacher check

1.35   Teacher check

1.36   Teacher check

1.37   Teacher check

1.38   true

1.39   true

1.40   false

1.41   true

1.42   false

1.43-1.51 Examples:

1.43   heavy night; wild shore

1.44   stirring drums

1.45   desert gloom; lofty cheer

1.46   sounding aisles; dim woods

1.47   rocking pines

1.48   hoary hair

1.49   fearless eye; deep love; serenely high; fiery heart

1.50   bright jewels

1.51   holy ground

1.52   b

SECTION ONE (cont.)

1.53 c

1.54 a

1.55 c

1.56 Example:
He was tough, careless, mean.

1.57 Example:
He has a nobler nature, too. He can be kind.

1.58 Example:
I disliked him.

1.59 Example:
I thought he might be all right if it were not war time.

1.60 Examples:
a. peacefulness
b. fear
c. excitement
d. dislike
or admiration, liking, patriotism, pride

1.61 add, add *i*, addition

1.62 attract, drop *t*, attraction

1.63 celebrate, drop *te*, celebration

1.64 separate, drop *te*, separation

1.65 suppose, drop *e*, add *i*, supposition

1.66 vacate, drop *te*, vacation

1.67 drop *y*, add *e*, beauteous

1.68 drop *on*, cautious

1.69 drop *le*, add *ul*, fabulous

1.70 drop *e*, add *i*, malicious

1.71 no change, scandalous

1.72 drop *on*, suspicious

1.73 Example:
We had ice cream cones afterward.

1.74 Example:
It is safer to ride facing backward.

1.75 Example:
Push the seat forward a little so you will be closer to the desk.

1.76 Example:
We were happy to turn homeward at the end of the day's work.

1.77 Example:
Look toward me so you can see my lips make the /b/ sound.

1.78 Example:
In the early days of the United States, people were moving westward.

1.79 very beautiful; full of beauty

1.80 using caution; being very careful

1.81 hardly believable; like a fable

1.82 full of bitterness; having malice

1.83 shameful; shocking

1.84 causing or having suspicion or distrust

1.85-1.90 Examples:

1.85 Brett was a welcome addition to the team.

1.86 The male quartet was quite an attraction at the school concert.

1.87 On grandfather's eightieth birthday we had a big celebration.

1.88 I do not like the separation from my friend when she goes away for the summer.

1.89 Be careful of ideas that are based on supposition instead of fact.

1.90 We are going to the lake for our vacation this year.

1.91 Teacher check

SECTION TWO

2.1 hun-, men, King, say
Ab-, kept, house, day
fif-, chains, -out, doubt
vel-, wait, Ab-, -bout

2.2 Any order:
a. King John
b. Abbot of Canterbury
c. the Abbot's shepherd

2.3 the shepherd

2.4 Any order:
a. "Tell to one penny what I am worth."
b. "How quickly may I ride the whole world about?"
c. "What do I think?"

2.5 cut off the Abbot's head

2.6 Either order:
a. Cambridge
b. Oxenford

2.7 Example:
The Abbot told his shepherd that King John had demanded the answer to three questions. If the Abbot could not answer the questions, he would be killed. The shepherd offered to dress as the Abbot and ride to London to answer King John. The Abbot agreed and gave to the shepherd everything he needed to make him look like the Abbot. Off rode the shepherd to London.

2.8 yes

2.9 as riddles

2.10 yes

2.11 He said he could neither read nor write.

2.12 a. He gave the shepherd four nobles a week.
b. He gave a pardon to the Abbot.

2.13 b

2.14 true
2.15 false
2.16 false
2.17 true
2.18 true
2.19 true
2.20 false
2.21 false
2.22 false
2.23 true
2.24 b
2.25 c
2.26 a
2.27 b
2.28 a
2.29 Dad
2.30 put up
2.31 Adam
2.32 Panama
2.33 Elba
2.34 a. bough
b. bow
2.35 a. oar
b. or
2.36 a. seer
b. sear
2.37 a. Peel
b. peal
2.38 a. bold
b. bowled
2.39 a. formerly
b. formally
2.40 a. latter
b. later
2.41 a. prophesy
b. prophecy
2.42 paddle
2.43 amount
2.44 ability
2.45 Teacher check

SECTION TWO (cont.)

2.46 office, position, or occupation of; quality or condition of being; act, power or skill; relation between

2.47 tending to; causing; to a considerable degree; group of (with a number)

2.48 Example:
The kittens were frolicsome.

2.49 Example:
The two small children were quarrelsome and fussy.

2.50 Example:
When you are a guest, you should help with the work so that you will not be burdensome.

2.51 Example:
The smelly garbage dump was a loathesome place.

2.52 Example:
Golf is a game you can play with a threesome.

2.53 a kinship or relationship

2.54 authorship or penmanship

2.55 friendship

2.56 an apprenticeship

2.57 statesmanship

2.58 Friend check

2.59 Teacher check

SECTION THREE

3.1-3.4 Examples:

3.1 Part 1 gives a description of how the blacksmith looks.

3.2 Part 2 has a description of the blacksmith at work.

3.3 Part 3 is a description of the blacksmith at church with his family.

3.4 Part 4 shows the lesson we learn from the kind of man the blacksmith is.

3.5 He doesn't owe anything to anyone.

3.6 His wife has died.

3.7 He enjoys sitting with his boys in church and hearing his daughter sing in the choir.

3.8 Example:
Work well done makes you sleep well at night.

3.9 Teacher check

3.10 Example:
The line means you don't know whether tomorrow will bring difficulty or happiness.

3.11 It means "whatever may come."

3.12 "Evening falls" and "earth's day grows dim" are symbols for the end of life. No one knows when the end of life will come.

3.13 a. "I do not know"
b. "I know"

3.14 She knows Christ abides within, His presence will hold her up, and God will call her to go to Heaven.

3.15-3.24 Examples:

3.15 lumberyard

3.16 elephant

3.17 cupcakes

3.18 panda bears

3.19 monkeys

3.20 whistle

3.21 grocery store

3.22 jump rope

3.23 penguin

3.24 crayons

3.25-3.29 Examples:

3.25   a monkey

3.26   a lady bug

3.27   a stung puppy

3.28   a windmill on a windless day

3.29   a brown bear at a garbage dump

3.30-3.34 Examples:

3.30   The traffic officer at the busy intersection was a windmill in a whirlwind.

3.31   The hiker with his backpack was a camel plodding far from an oasis.

3.32   Cars on a freeway at night are hundreds of shooting stars.

3.33   Children coming out of school are marbles spilling and bouncing on the walk.

3.34   The lawn water sprinkler became a silver plume, rainbow-colored in the sunlight.

3.35   dashed high

3.36   tossed

3.37   heard

3.38   looked down

3.39   tossed

3.40   loved it well

3.41   draw round thy symbol of light and law

3.42   look down

3.43   roar or blow

3.44   flew up and down

3.45   e

3.46   b

3.47   a

3.48   d and e

3.49   c

3.50   e

3.51   Teacher check

3.52   Teacher check

3.53   The Shell

3.54   whorl, pink, cream

3.55   secret, sound, sea

3.56   whorl, cream, sea, dream

3.57   The sound of the sea.

3.58   Teacher check

3.59   working clothes

3.60   grass, or green crops

3.61   throws away

3.62   the crop has been gathered

3.63   the bare earth

3.64   brooch

3.65   noticed by someone who may come along

3.66   lonely people and the things they sometimes do in order to be noticed

3.67   Teacher check

3.68   Teacher check

3.69   true

3.70   false

3.71   false

3.72   true

3.73   true

3.74   false

3.75   false

3.76   true

3.77   Teacher check

3.78   halves

3.79   shelves

3.80   beliefs

3.81   chiefs

3.82   handkerchiefs

3.83   a

3.84   a

3.85   b

3.86   a

3.87   a

3.88   b

3.89   a

3.90   a

3.91   b

3.92   Teacher check

SECTION ONE

1.1   a. The hurricane caused the wreck.

       b. They decided to build their next home in the mountains and never build on the beach again.

1.2   a. The missionary applied medicine to the skin.

       b. It cleared up the disease.

1.3   a. He cured the children of the skin disease.

       b. The people, especially the children, listened to his Bible stories.

1.4   complexion

1.5   inventory

1.6   plague

1.7   voyage

1.8   potion

1.9   famished

1.10 contraption

1.11 substance

1.12 transparent

1.13 ointment

1.14 debate

1.15 shrill

1.16 wrench

1.17 loin

1.18 embroider

1.19 inhabitant

1.20 perceive

1.21 venture

1.22 mingle

1.23 a. 2
       b. 1
       c. 4
       d. 5
       e. 3

       f. 6

1.24 a. 2
       b. 4
       c. 3
       d. 5
       e. 10
       f. 8
       g. 6
       h. 9
       i. 7

1.25 c. Jonathan Swift

1.26 a. six inches tall

1.27 a. shot arrows at Gulliver

1.28 c. by a horse-pulled cart with twenty-two wheels

1.29 b. chained to a ruined temple

1.30 b. was green with forests and fields

1.31 c. spoke an entirely new language he could not understand

1.32 b. to feed and clothe Gulliver

1.33 a. assisted the two searchers

1.34 a. was delighted

1.35 The little people climbed on him.

1.36 He roared loudly.

1.37 He moved.

1.38 The little people shot him with arrows

1.39 Several officers spoke favorably to the council about Gulliver.

1.40 Gulliver received food and drink.

1.41 The horse pawed his foot and ripped a hole in the handkerchief.

1.42 The horse slipped and overthrew the rider.

1.43 Gulliver wrote many letters asking for his freedom.

1.44 The king mentioned his freedom to the council.

1.45 Teacher check
1.46 Teacher check
1.47 Teacher check
1.48 Teacher check
1.49 Teacher check
1.50 Teacher check

1.51
Down	Across
1. sight	2. cite
4. night	3. knight
5. hire	5. higher
6. idol	6. idle
7. aisle	8. isle
9. size	10. sighs
11. prize	12. pries
13. pried	14. pride
15. fined	15. find
16. minor	16. miner

1.52 pried
1.53 pries
1.54 Either order:
   a. mine
   b. high
1.55 Any order:
   a. knight
   b. prize
   c. isle
   or night, miner, minor, sight,
   pride, idol, aisle, size

1.56 Any order:
   a. find
   b. pried
   c. hire
   or cite, sighs, pries, fined, sight

1.57 Cross out night. Write knight.
   Cross out idol. Write idle.
   Cross out pries. Write prize.
   Cross out cite. Write sight.
   Cross out minor. Write miner.
   Cross out higher. Write hire.
   Cross out aisle. Write isle.
   Cross out pried.   Write pride.
   Cross out fined. Write find.
   Cross out night. Write knight.
   Cross out sighs. Write size.

1.58 Teacher check
1.59 Teacher check

SECTION TWO

2.1   coconut, foreman, mechanic, grape-
        vine, cactus, emperor, magnet

2.2-2.11   Examples:

2.2   man or woman or person

2.3   deer

2.4   bear

2.5   post office

2.6   church

2.7   janitor

2.8   clock

2.9   wheat

2.10   plane

2.11   bags

2.12   Maple Street

2.13   Jehovah

2.14   Arizona

2.15   Atlantic Ocean

2.16   General Smith

2.17   England

2.18   Golden Gate Bridge

2.19   Bryan College

2.20   Mr. Thomas

2.21   Laura Ingalls Wilder

2.22-2.27   Examples:

2.22   Mrs. Jones

2.23   Rocky Mountains

2.24   Arizona

2.25   Tempe

2.26   Atlantic Ocean

2.27   First Baptist Church

2.28   4

2.29   3

2.30   1

2.31   2

2.32   P

2.33   S

2.34   P

2.35   P

2.36   S

2.37   skies

2.38   monkeys

2.39   chickens

2.40   oxen

2.41   pickles

2.42-2.50   Examples:

2.42   bird

2.43   boy

2.44   man

2.45   roof

2.46   child

2.47   mouse

2.48   river

2.49   lake

2.50   pioneer

2.51   Teacher check

2.52   The boy's suit is mended.

2.53   The referee's whistle is broken.

2.54   The cook's meal is delicious.

2.55   The man's key is missing.

2.56   The baby's toys were cute.

2.57   The babies' cradles were handmade.

2.58   The monkeys' cage was repaired.

2.59   The senators' speeches were long.

2.60   The children's bus was late.

2.61   The men's jobs were difficult.

2.62   The kittens' paws were white.

2.63   The sheep's pasture was flooded.

2.64   The teachers' books arrived early.

2.65 reindeer's

2.66 disciples'

2.67 mother's

2.68 oxen's

2.69 zoo's

2.70 girls, (circus)

2.71 river, (and)

2.72 fire, (building)

2.73 composer, (music)

2.74 man, (cereal)

2.75 Alan (bicycle)

2.76 minister, (Bible)

2.77 logger, (timber)

2.78 daisy, (flower)

2.79 boy, (bike)

2.80-2.84 Examples:

2.80 The boy petted the (dog.)

2.81 Alice cleaned the (floor.)

2.82 The painter painted a (picture)

2.83 The girl read a (book.)

2.84 Peter was a (fisherman.)

2.85 She

2.86 It

2.87 They

2.88 We

2.89 He

2.90 He

2.91 its

2.92 Their

2.93 their

2.94 her

2.95 his

2.96-2.100 Examples:

2.96 our

2.97 Her

2.98 their

2.99 your

2.100 my

2.101 Teacher check

2.102 Teacher check

2.103 Either order:

    a. insure

    b. surely

2.104 Any order:

    a issue

    b. mission

    c. pressure

2.105 Any order:

    a. chef

    b. chute

    c. machinery

2.106 Any order:

    a. education

    b. emotion

    c. fiction

    d. lotion

    e. solution

    f. vacation

2.107 Either order:

    a. suspicious

    b. vicious

2.108
    a. education   f. machinery

    b. solution   g. chef

    c. vicious   h. vision

    d. pressure   i. issue

    e. mission   j. measure

2.109 d

    e

    i

    c

    h

    b

    j

    f

    a

    g

SECTION TWO (cont.)

2.110   Teacher check

2.111   yawn

       valley

       water

wood

villain

whistle

yellow

SECTION THREE

3.1	wrong	3.11	F
3.2	right	3.12	O
3.3	right	3.13	F
3.4	wrong	3.14	F
3.5	Example:	3.15	O
	Yes, the Bible tells us we	3.16	F
	are to obey God rather than	3.17	O
	men. God has told parents to	3.18	a. fearful
	train up their children in the	3.19	b. sorrowful
	way they should go. That way	3.20	c. joyful
	is to know Jesus Christ as	3.21	tense
	Saviour. Acts 5:28 and 29,	3.22	instigator
	Proverbs 22:6	3.23	purge
3.6	Example:	3.24	martyr
	Yes, Ann should obey her parents.	3.25	persecution
	Ephesians 6:1 and 2, tells us to	3.26	refuge
	obey our parents and to honor our	3.27	bitter
	father and mother. By being	3.28	c. Jesus helped Marc forgive his
	obedient, Ann may be a witness to		enemy, Saul.
	her parents.	3.29	a. about sixty-five A.D., when the
3.7	Example:		church was young.
	The Professor stepped into the	3.30	c. father, mother, and one brother.
	time machine, and this time it	3.31	b. a gentle woman but very ill.
	worked. He disappeared into	3.32	b. confessed Jesus as the Son of
	another time period.		God.
3.8	Example:	3.33	a. escaped.
	The riders did not lasso Susan's	3.34	c. the "cave people."
	favorite stallion. He got away	3.35	a. died in prison.
	and was still free.	3.36	b. his father died.
3.9	O	3.37	c. Saul.
3.10	F	3.38	a. in prison.

3.39 b. forgave Paul.
3.40 c. left prison to go to a faraway
          village to settle and preach the
          Gospel.
3.41 No. He stole food. The Bible tells
      us not to steal.
3.42 Yes. They did not want to eat
      food they knew was stolen.
3.43 No. He lied to the soldiers.
3.44 Yes. They did not lie and they did not
      beytray the "cave people."
3.45 Example:
      The family was thrown into prison.
3.46 Example:
      The boy went to live with Cyrenius.
      He became one of his family.
3.47 O
3.48 F
3.49 O
3.50 F
3.51 b. excitement
3.52 a. fear
3.53 Teacher check

3.54 a. bought   f. naught
      b. fought   g. slaughter
      c. sought   h. thoughtful
      d. taught   i. cough
      e. caught   j. naughty
3.55 a. bought   d. taught
      b. sought   e. caught
      c. fought
3.56 cough
3.57 conquer
3.58 vacuum
3.59 biscuit
3.60 disguise
3.61 Either order:
      a. emperor
      b. worship
3.62 a. physical
      b. rhythm
3.63 a. I rode a stallion.
      b. We ate at a restaurant.
3.64 Teacher check
3.65 Teacher check
3.66 Teacher check

SECTION FOUR

4.1   sour, kind, large, cold, small, tough, warm, green

4.2-4.11   Examples:

4.2   big

4.3   hungry

4.4   wild

4.5   sweet

4.6   blue

4.7   lost

4.8   yellow

4.9   hot

4.10   soft

4.11   fresh

4.12-4.15   Examples:

4.12   I have a new bike.

4.13   The young boy walked home.

4.14   She wore an attractive dress.

4.15   He has a bad cough.

4.16-4.20   Examples:

4.16   Many

4.17   several

4.18   five

4.19   few

4.20   twenty

4.21   The little boy carried a big, brass tuba.

4.22   The busy beaver cut down a small tree.

4.23   The old, dark shack was filled with dirty, old papers.

4.24   The clear, mild weather was perfect for a good baseball game.

4.25   The new queen heard the sad news.

4.26-4.35   Examples:

4.26   strong

4.27   long

4.28   beautiful

4.29   green

4.30   hungry

4.31   bright

4.32   tall

4.33   old

4.34   tired

4.35   hard

4.36   room, dark

4.37   desert, dry

4.38   machine, broken

4.39   boy, scout

4.40   summer, long

4.41   sparrow, bird

4.42   hammer, tool

4.43   rose, beautiful

4.44   rose, flower

4.45   man, banker

4.46-4.51   Examples:

4.46   The little boy walked to his big farm house.

4.47   The hungry wolf ran into the dark forest.

4.48   The clever magician fooled the silly people.

4.49   The kind girl visited an old, dear friend.

4.50   The little old man begged for a little food.

4.51   Example:
The frightened boy ran into the deep forest. The deep forest was full of giant trees, clinging vines, and wild animals. He looked for a good place to hide. In a small cave, he found a growling wolf. The lonely wolf was a hurt animal that needed some help. The brave boy helped the wounded wolf. The grateful wolf became his faithful friend.

4.52   Teacher check

4.53   a. bough   f. though
       b. drought   g. thorough
       c. dough   h. tough
       d. doughnut   i. rough
       e. throughout   j. laugh

4.54   pierce

160

4.55   Any order:
- a. kerchief
- b. brief
- c. grief
- d. shriek

4.56   neigh

4.57   Either order:
- a. assign, or throughout, bough, drought, dough, doughnut, though, thorough, neigh
- b. limb

4.58   weapon

4.59   embarrass

4.60   bough, drought, or rough

4.61
- a. kerchief
- b. brief
- c. grief
- d. pierce
- e. shriek
- f. weapon
- g. neigh
- h. assign
- i. limb
- j. embarrass

4.62   Teacher check

4.63   Teacher check

SECTION ONE

1.1

1.2 sold

1.3 planned

1.4 skated

1.5 grazed

1.6
  a. action
  b. being
  c. being
  d. being
  e. action
  f. action
  g. action
  h. action
  i. being
  j. action
  k. being
  l. action

1.7 Any order:
  a. sinned
  b. disobeyed
  c. prayed
  d. confessed
  e. worshipped
  f. created
  g. redeemed
  h. loved
  i. forgave

1.8-1.17 Examples:

1.8 obey

1.9 shouted

1.10 cry

1.11 bark

1.12 dismissed

1.13 orbited

1.14 walked

1.15 destroyed

1.16 opened

1.17 raced

1.18 Teacher check

1.19-1.27 Examples:

1.19 tell

1.20 obey

1.21 play

1.22 talk

1.23 wash or dry

1.24 clean

1.25 read

1.26 worship or praise

1.27 write

1.28 created, past, regular

1.29 talked, past, regular

1.30 chose, past, irregular

1.31 provided, past, regular

1.32 died, past, regular

1.33 rose, past, irregular

1.34 asked, past, regular

1.35 will return, future, regular

1.36 is, present, irregular

1.37 saves, present, regular

1.38 will return, future, regular

1.39 shared, past, regular

1.40 d

1.41 Examples:
  a. My mother (baked) a birthday cake for Jimmy.
  b. Dad and mother (go) to prayer meeting on Wednesday nights.
  c. The football coach (said) the team played hard.
  d. This time of year (is) the best.
  e. Janice (played) tennis with Marilyn today.

1.42 am
1.43 were
1.44 were
1.45 was
1.46 are
1.47 are
1.48 a. was
      b. were
1.49 was
1.50 were
1.51 was
1.52 aren't
1.53 wasn't
1.54 You're
1.55 hasn't
1.56 won't
1.57 It's
1.58 I'm
1.59 i
1.60 a
1.61 j
1.62 c
1.63 e
1.64 b
1.65 d
1.66 f
1.67 g

1.68 was skiing
1.69 will be singing
1.70 was studying
1.71 were going
1.72 marching, sleeping, pounding, stomping, hiding, watching, rapping, frightened, praying
1.73 is
1.74 aren't
1.75 were
1.76 are
1.77 are
1.78 isn't
1.79 were
1.80 isn't
1.81 was
1.82 are
1.83 is
1.84 wasn't
1.85 ain't
1.86 ain't
1.87 are
1.88 exposure
1.89 closure
1.90 failure
1.91 mixture
1.92 pleasure
1.93 pressure
1.94 moisture
1.95 legislature
1.96 measure or pressure
1.97 stature
1.98 rapture
1.99 structure
1.100 fracture
1.101 Scripture
1.102 procedure
1.103 literature
1.104 Teacher check

SECTION TWO

2.1	c
2.2	2
2.3	6
2.4	5
2.5	4
2.6	1
2.7	3
2.8	8
2.9	7
2.10	9
2.11	Teacher check
2.12	Examples:

    a. The Lion and the Mouse – Everyone has worth.

    b. The Dog and the Bone – Greediness doesn't pay.

    c. The Wind and the Sun – Persuasion is better than force.

    d. The Hare and the Tortoise – Persistence wins the race.

2.13	a. slave
	b. stories
2.14	India
2.15	fables
2.16	fictitious
2.17	moral
2.18	imaginary, made up
2.19	directed attention
2.20	laziness
2.21	unexpectedly met, experienced
2.22	suggested without actually saying it
2.23	rule to follow

2.24	charged money
2.25	got off
2.26	Teacher check
2.27	Teacher check
2.28	Teacher check
2.29	Teacher check
2.30	marriage
2.31	carriage
2.32	usage
2.33	storage
2.34	shrinkage
2.35	stoppage
2.36	supervision
2.37	illusion
2.38	allusion
2.39	intercession
2.40	conclusion
2.41	~~weigh~~; way
2.42	~~wade~~; weighed
2.43	~~Waist~~; Waste
2.44	~~weight~~; wait
2.45	~~vains~~; veins
2.46	~~tale~~; tail
2.47	weighed
2.48	waste
2.49	vain
2.50	way
2.51	Teacher check
2.52	Teacher check
2.53	Teacher check

SECTION THREE

3.1 cautiously began

3.2 burst noisily

3.3 was now running

3.4 pushed hard

3.5 is here

3.6 perfectly pitched

3.7 really great

3.8 specially good

3.9 fairly clean

3.10 badly torn

3.11 too or very

3.12 quite, too, or very

3.13 extremely or very

3.14 very

3.15 perfectly or extremely

3.16 hurriedly swept - verb

3.17 patiently waited - verb

3.18 truly courageous - adjective

3.19 very softly - adverb
softly sang - verb

3.20 swiftly ran - verb

3.21 specially bright - adjective
clearly shone - verb

3.22 lovingly provided - verb

3.23 quietly thinking - adjective

3.24 diligently sought - verb

3.25 very wicked - adjective

3.26 loudly

3.27 nicely

3.28 swiftly

3.29 quickly

3.30 cheerfully

3.31 truthfully

3.32 neatly

3.33 crazily

3.34 carelessly

3.35 interestingly

3.36 boldly

3.37 kindly

3.38 cautiously

3.39 gloriously

3.40 swiftly

3.41 carefully

3.42 joyfully

3.43 selfishly

3.44 sweetly

3.45 generously

3.46 Examples:
  a. wearily
  b. beautifully
  c. Suddenly
  d. quickly
  e. angrily
  f. tiredly, ploddingly
  g. kindly
  h. very
  i. heavily
  j. anxiously
  k. Impatiently, Instantly
  l. gently
  m. quickly
  n. unusually
  o. extremely
  p. Excitedly
  q. softly, dimly
  r. strangely
  s. silently
  t. surely
  u. Quietly
  v. humbly

3.47 often

3.48 more often

3.49 most often

3.50 well

3.51 better

3.52 best

3.53 fast

3.54 faster

3.55 fastest

3.56 Example:
My friends have never found an elephant.

SECTION THREE (cont.)

3.57 Example:
There is nothing better than to
find a true friend.

3.58 Example:
I could hardly find an elephant
for a true friend.

3.59 Example:
I have never had any opportunities
to look for an elephant.

3.60 Example:
I have never been offered an elephant.

3.61 a. barely
c. most
d. sleepily
i. sweetly
j. anywhere
l. scarcely
m. no
n. never
o. really
p. soon
q. fully
r. here
s. not
t. often

3.62 Adverbs limit the meaning of words
that express action by telling how,
when, or where.

3.63 Adverbs also modify adjectives
and adverbs.

3.64 Some adjectives are changed to
adverbs by adding *-ly* to the
adjective.

3.65 When adverbs modify verbs, they
answer the questions how, when,
and where.

3.66 a. Adverbs modify verbs, adjectives, and adverbs.
b. Adverbs modify verbs by an-
swering the question of how,
when, and where.

c. Adverbs modify adjectives to
tell you more about adjectives.
d. Adverbs modify adverbs by
making the meaning of the
adverbs more precise.

3.67 The three degrees of comparison
are positive, comparative, and
superlative.

3.68 a. Positive-basic form of the
word-simply modifies.
b. Comparative-compares two things.
c. Superlative-compares more than
two things.

3.69 Any order:
a. by adding *-er* or *-est*
b. by using *more* and *most*
c. by using *well*, *better*, or
best

3.70 Adverbs that express negative
meaning are negative adverbs.

3.71 The words *not* and *no* are negative
and it is incorrect to use more
than one negative in a sentence.

3.72 Wyoming scarcely got any snow.

3.73 The wind hardly blows in Arizona.

3.74 We haven't ever had a blizzard.

3.75 School children don't miss class
when it snows in Minnesota.

3.76 We didn't do anything the day of
the storm.

3.77 comical

3.78 musical

3.79 electrical

3.80 editorial

3.81 financial

3.82 congressional

3.83 racial

3.84 intellectual

3.85 contractual

3.86 spiritual

3.87 eventual

3.88   burial

3.89   commercial

3.90   industrial

3.91   presidential

3.92   Clerical

3.93   Musical

3.94   Comical

3.95   electrical

3.96   Financial

3.97   editorial

3.98   Congressional

3.99   racial

3.100 intellectual

3.101 contractual

3.102 spiritual

3.103 eventual

3.104 burial

3.105 Commercial

3.106 Industrial

3.107 Presidential

3.108 Teacher check

SECTION ONE

1.1	b.	scientific truths
1.2	a.	Jeremiah
1.3	a.	1,056
1.4	b.	seventeenth
1.5	c.	two thousand to three thousand
1.6	a.	one hundred billion
1.7	c.	millions of
1.8	a.	cannot number
1.9		charity
1.10		2
1.11		b
1.12		a
1.13		c
1.14		a
1.15		b
1.16		Dick Whittington
1.17		Old England
1.18		500 years
1.19		three times
1.20		yes
1.21		Many people believe the cat was real.
1.22		Halloway
1.23		a
1.24		a
1.25		b
1.26		c
1.27		b
1.28		a
1.29		b
1.30		a
1.31		b
1.32		2
		5
		1
		7
		4
		10
		6
		8
		3

	12
	13
	9
	14
	15
	11
1.33	The cat chased away the mice.
1.34	Example:
	The captain took the cat on his ship and Dick missed her.
1.35	Example:
	The captain went to the ship to get the cat and returned.
1.36	Example:
	After the cat took care of the mice, she climbed into the queen's lap.
1.37	Example:
	The captain knocked on the door, and Mr. Fitzwarren answered it.
1.38	a
1.39	c
1.40	b
1.41	a
1.42	Teacher check
1.43	Any order:

1.43 (continued)

a. a/ban/don
b. a/broad
c. a/brupt
d. ac/count
e. a/dopt
f. al/low
g. ap/par/ent
h. ap/pren/tice
i. a/quar/i/um
j. at/tach

1.44   Any order:
    a. broad/side
    b. fire/place
    c. grape/vine
    d. hard/ship
    e. team/mate

1.45   Any order:
    a. pup/pet
    b. ras/cal
    c. rep/tile
    d. rug/ged
    e. wit/ness

1.46   a. abroad
    b. account
    c. adopt
    d. abandon
    e. apparent
    f. aquarium
    g. apprentice
    h. attach
    i. allow
    j. abrupt

1.47   ged, cal, tile
    pet, ness

1.48   Examples:
    a. The car was hit broadside in the accident.
    b. His teammate was the fastest runner in the school.
    c. It was a hardship for the pioneers to cross the mountains.
    d. Jane's grapevine produced the juiciest grapes in the valley.
    e. They gathered around the fireplace to pop popcorn.

1.49   Teacher check

1.50   Examples:
    a. Al Alligator
    b. Bobbie Bear
    c. Connie Codfish
    d. Dilly Dog
    e. Edgar Eel
    f. Floppy Fish
    g. Gilbert Guinea Pig
    h. Itsy Insect
    i. Jolly Jaguar
    j. Lazy Lizard
    k. Ollie Octopus
    l. Polly Parakeet
    m. Randy Raccoon
    n. Sammy Seal
    o. Tilly Tiger

SECTION TWO

2.1   yes

2.2   Either order:
    a. the Pacific Ocean
    b. the Indian Ocean

2.3   long

2.4   Example:
Australia is completely surrounded by water. Asia is bordered by another continent. Australia is smaller in size. Asia is in the Northern Hemisphere or above the equator. Australia is in the Southern Hemisphere or below the equator.

2.5   Either order:
White shark and Ganges River shark

2.6   Either order:
White shark and Tiger shark

2.7   Ganges River shark

2.8   white

2.9   Either order:
Porbeagle shark and the White-tipped shark

2.10   93 million miles

2.11   Mercury

2.12   nine

2.13   no

2.14   Either order:
Jupiter and Saturn

2.15   Pluto

2.16   three

2.17   You hold the tube securely and then scratch it with a triangular file.

2.18   the thumb

2.19   You hold the tube over the flame until the sharp edges melt.

2.20   Teacher check

2.21   no

2.22   Bascule bridges

2.23   yes

2.24
  I. Farmer Ants That Plant Crops
    A. Chew leaves until mushy
    B. Put mush in homes
    C. Plant mushroom spores in mush
  II. Ants That Have Dairy Farms
    A. Milk insects called aphids
    B. Carry cows from place to place
  III. Ants That Store Food for Others
    A. Stuff themselves with honey
    B. Are hanging honeypots
    C. Supply hungry ants with a drink

2.25
  I. How a Duckbill Platypus Looks
    A. Has a bill like a duck
    B. Has grayish-brown fur
    C. Has a flattened tail
    D. Has webbed feet
  II. How a Duckbill Platypus Lays Her Eggs
    A. Digs a den
    B. Lays two or three eggs
    C. Seals them together
    D. Holds eggs closely to chest, rolls into a ball until hatched
  III. What a Baby Platypus Is Like
    A. Blind until four months old
    B. Has no fur until two months old
    C. Born with strange little bills
    D. Is friendly and playful

2.26   Haman and the king (or King Ahasuerus)

2.27   He was afraid.

2.28   Outline Of Esther
  I. Esther Made Queen
    A. Maidens were brought to the palace for king's selection of a queen
    B. Mordecai the Jew sent his cousin Esther
    C. Esther was chosen queen

II. Haman Made a Plot
  A. King commanded servants to bow to Haman
  B. Jewish Mordecai would not bow to Haman
  C. Furious Haman sent orders to kill all Jews
III. Esther Showed Courage
  A. Mordecai asked Esther to go before the king
  B. Esther risked her life going before the king
  C. Esther invited Haman and the king to a banquet
  D. Esther revealed Haman's plot at the second banquet
IV. Justice Was Accomplished
  A. Haman was hanged
  B. Mordecai was given position of authority
  C. A new decree allowed Jews to gather and defend themselves

2.29 Examples:

Young maidens were brought to the palace for the king to select a new queen. Mordecai the Jew sent his cousin Esther. Esther pleased the king and was chosen to be queen.

The king commanded all his servants to bow down to Haman, but Jewish Mordecai would not bow down to him. Haman was furious and sent orders for all Jews to be killed.

Mordecai asked Queen Esther to go before the king. Risking her own life, she went before the king and invited the king and Haman to a banquet. At the second banquet, Esther revealed Haman's evil plot to kill the Jews.

Haman was then hanged. Mordecai was given a position of authority. A new decree was issued to allow Jews to gather and defend themselves.

2.30 teacher check
2.31 Any order:
  a. alley
  b. jersey
  c. valley
2.32 Either order:
  a. delight
  b. midnight
2.33 Either order:
  a. guard
  b. guide
2.34 hymn
2.35 Either order:
  a. wrist
  b. wrong
2.36 Any order:
  a. clothes
  b. exercise
  c. jersey
  d. pleasant
  e. president or suppose
2.37 Any order:
  a. battle
  b. crumble
  c. fatal
  d. hospital
  e. nickel
2.38 clothes
  exercise
  president
  suppose
  pleasant
2.39 fatal
  battle
  hospital
  nickel
  crumble

SECTION TWO (cont.)

2.40 a. valley
b. midnight
c. wrong
d. guard
e. jersey
f. alley
g. wrist

2.41 Delight

2.42 Example:
have pleasure in

2.43 Example:
I can enjoy my time with Him in prayer.

2.44 guide
hymn

2.45 teacher check

2.46 Examples:
Hawaii
Uruguay
Kentucky
Venezuela
Norway
Yugoslavia
Quebec
Washington
New Zealand

SECTION THREE

3.1 SS

3.2 SS

3.3 N

3.4 N

3.5 N

3.6 SS

3.7 N

3.8 textbook

3.9 magazine article

3.10 nursery rhyme

3.11 drama

3.12 newspaper

3.13 history

3.14 poem

3.15 poetry

3.16 short story

3.17 history

3.18 biography or short story

3.19 Literature is the body of writings of a period, language, or country especially those writings kept alive by their beauty or effectiveness of style or thought.

3.20 Examples:
a. The distance from San Francisco to Australia is seventy-six hundred miles.
b. Captain James Cook discovered Australia in 1770.
c. The British sent convicts to colonize Australia.
or the official name of Australia is The Commonwealth of Australia; Australia is the world's largest island; Australia is approximately the size of the United States; Australia's Aborigines live in the interior deserts.

3.21 Examples:
a. No other country in the world has such unusual animals.
b. The strangest animal is the platypus.
c. The country is very interesting and beautiful.
or Some of the world's most beautiful beaches are in Australia; The way of life is slower; Australians have a natural confidence and acceptance of life.

3.22   Example:
       My Trip to Hawaii
3.23   Example:
       encyclopedia, Sunset Book on Hawaii
3.24   teacher check
3.25   <u>Down</u>
       1. reel
       2. beach
       3. knead
       5. creek
       6. feet
       7. peace
       8. steel
       9. peal
       10. peer
       11. flea
       <u>Across</u>
       1. real
       2. beech
       4. need
       5. creak
       6. feat
       7. piece
       8. steal
       9. peel
       10. pier
       11. flee
3.26   Any order:
       a. beach
       b. flea
       c. reel
       d. beech
       e. feet
       f. steel
       g. creek
       h. peel
       i. pier
       or peace, need, feat, piece, peal, steal

3.27   Any order:
       a. creak
       b. need
       c. steal
       d. flee
       e. knead
       or peal, reel, peer, peel, beach, piece
3.28   beach
3.29   beech
3.30   flee
3.31   flea
3.32   creek
3.33   creak
3.34   feet
3.35   feat
3.36   need
3.37   knead
3.38   steal
3.39   steel
3.40   reel
3.41   real
3.42   pier
3.43   peer
3.44   peace
3.45   piece
3.46   peel
3.47   peal
3.48   Teacher check
3.49   Teacher check

SECTION ONE

1.1	1, 3, 4
1.2	1, 2, 3, 4, 5
1.3	2, 3, 6
1.4	1, 2, 5
1.5	not good
1.6	good
1.7	good
1.8	not good
1.9	c
1.10	d
1.11	b
1.12	e
1.13	L
1.14	SS
1.15	N
1.16	P
1.17	D
1.18	N
1.19	F
1.20	D
1.21	NF
1.22	L
1.23	SS
1.24	NF
1.25	false
1.26	false
1.27	true
1.28	true
1.29	false
1.30	g
1.31	b
1.32	h
1.33	f
1.34	d
1.35	a
1.36	e
1.37	c
1.38	i
1.39	j
1.40	d
1.41	e
1.42	a
1.43	h

1.44	f
1.45	b
1.46	g
1.47	c
1.48	c
1.49	a
1.50	d
1.51	b
1.52	policeman, bakery, bottle, sword, newspaper, climber
1.53-1.57	Examples:
1.53	bank
1.54	squirrel
1.55	glass
1.56	radio
1.57	mechanic
1.58	France
1.59	Pacific Ocean
1.60	Baker Road
1.61	Mrs. Thomas
1.62	First Bible Church
1.63	P
1.64	P
1.65	S
1.66	P
1.67	S
1.68	babies
1.69	geese
1.70	monkeys
1.71	fish
1.72	branches
1.73	men's
1.74	oxen's
1.75	kittens'
1.76	train's
1.77	traders'
1.78	lion's
1.79	The roaring <u>river</u> flooded the valley.
1.80	The young <u>girl</u> found a lost puppy.
1.81	The <u>fireman</u> climbed the ladder.
1.82	The <u>pianist</u> found her music.

1.83 The <u>class</u> went to the (library)

1.84 He

1.85 They

1.86 She

1.87 We

1.88 its

1.89 her

1.90 their
Clues to find the squire at the castle:
P, S, fish, He, She, its

1.91 loud, green, happy, soft, many, sad, tall, raging

1.92 <u>The</u> <u>busy</u> beaver built <u>a</u> <u>sturdy</u> dam.

1.93 <u>The</u> dog is <u>hungry</u>.

1.94 <u>The</u> <u>dark</u> room was <u>scary</u>.

1.95 <u>A</u> <u>small</u> tree was planted by <u>the</u> <u>winding</u> stream.

1.96 <u>The</u> rose is <u>beautiful</u>.

1.97-1.99 Examples:

1.97 A hungry, green giant met a timid, frightened mouse.

1.98 The thirsty boy was lost in the hot, dry desert.

1.99 The wounded wolf hid in the dark cave.

1.100 Teacher check

1.101 Teacher check

1.102 Teacher check

1.103 a. ou, moun, tain, mountain
b. ou, a, bound, abound
c. ow, cow, ard, coward
d. ow, tow, er, tower
e. oi, boil, ing, boiling
f. oi, poi, son, poison
g. oy, roy, al, royal
h. oy, voy, age, voyage
i. ea, crea, ture, creature
j. au, cau, tion, caution
k. ee, free, dom, freedom
l. ay, pray, ing, praying
m. oo, book, let, booklet
n. ai, fail, ure, failure

1.104 Any order:
a. arrange

b. college
c. mistake
d. secure
e. suppose
f. treasure
or creature, failure, voyage

1.105 a. afternoon
b. hardship
c. brand-new
d. inlet
e. childhood
f. landscape
g. moonlight

1.106 a. believe
b. busy
c. doctor
d. business
e. raise
f. separate

1.107 a. haven't
b. won't
c. she'll
d. you're
e. we'd
f. should've
g. you've

1.108 a. automatic
b. betrayal
c. available
d. leadership
e. underneath
f. exceedingly

1.109 a. cha(l)k
b. fli(gh)t
c. glis(t)en
d. (k)neel
e. si(gh)
f. (w)res(t)(l)e

1.110 a. fact
b. deny
c. encourage
d. advance

1.111 Teacher check

SECTION TWO

2.1   Example:
        He probably wrote the story to
        entertain.

2.2   Example:
        Yes, because he had been a sailor,
        explored the South Pacific, and
        listened to his great-grandfather
        tell of his adventures as a sea
        captain in the South Seas.

2.3   You can't please everyone.

2.4   I. On the road and bridge to the
            market town
        II. Farmer, son, donkey, girls, elderly,
            gentlemen, women, and farmers
       III. Example:
            The farmer and his son were on
            their way to market to sell their
            donkey when they were met by
            several groups of people who
            criticized them for the way they
            managed the donkey. Finally, the
            donkey decided he had had enough
            and went home.

2.5   a. 5
        b. 1
        c. 2
        d. 4
        e. 6
        f. 3
        g. 8
        h. 7

2.6   Example:
        They probably wanted to protect
        themselves in case he decided to use
        the knife or pistols to harm them.

2.7   Example:
        She meant that she would probably
        be killed if she went before the

king uncalled.

2.8   Example:
        The queen left the king and went
        to prepare the banquet.

2.9   Example:
        She believed the serpent rather
        than God, and disobeyed God.

2.10   Example:.
        She ate the fruit and shared it
        with Adam.

2.11   wrong

2.12   right

2.13   wrong

2.14   wrong

2.15   F

2.16   F

2.17   O

2.18   F

2.19   O

2.20   O

2.21   sil'

2.22   three

2.23   syllable

2.24   three

2.25   five

2.26   abbreviation

2.27   b

2.28   e

2.29   f

2.30   c

2.31   g

2.32   d

2.33   a

2.34   Examples:
        a. John got cold feet and would not
            talk to Kristi.
        b. Harold did not know the answer so
            he beat around the bush.

2.35 Examples:
  a. The boy had to wind his watch again.
  b. The wind is blowing.
  c. We record all the information in this book.
  d. She played her new record album.
  e. Please read me a story.
  f. She read the book yesterday.
2.36 a. action
  b. being
  c. action
  d. action
  e. being
  f. being
  g. action
  h. being
  i. being
  j. action
  k. action
  l. action
2.37-2.41 Examples:
2.37 argued
2.38 is
2.39 slipped
2.40 were
2.41 chopped
2.42 brought, past, irregular
2.43 cleaned, past, regular
2.44 will return, future, regular
2.45 prayed, past, regular
2.46 share, present, regular
2.47 sold, past, irregular
2.48 is, present, irregular
2.49 will pray, future, regular
2.50 am
2.51 were

2.52 is
2.53 are
2.54 was
2.55 are studying
2.56 will be going
2.57 was bowling
2.58 is buying
2.59 was sold
2.60 raging, scared, hiding, concerned, pounding, praying, sleeping
2.61 quietly
2.62 there
2.63 cautiously
2.64 perfectly
2.65 quickly
2.66 extremely radiant
2.67 really great
2.68 fairly heavy
2.69 neatly organized
2.70 rapidly deteriorating
2.71-2.73 Examples:
2.71 quite
2.72 too
2.73 very
2.74 swiftly
2.75 sleepily
2.76 brightly
2.77 clearly
2.78 carelessly
2.79 well
2.80 better
2.81 best
2.82-2.84 Examples:
2.82 never
2.83 scarcely
2.84 hardly

SECTION TWO (cont.)

2.85 a. n
      b. k, e
      c. t
      d. c,e
      e. t, e
      f. h

2.86 a. f
      b. gh
      c. ph

2.87 Either order: Any order:
      a. celery   c. castle
      b. citizen   d. compliment
                    e. confident
                    f. cough
                      or cucumber

2.88 a. boarder, border
      b. oar, or
      c. pair, pear

2.89 Across   Down
      3. employment   1. amazement
      4. materialism   2. realism
      6. Americanism   5. restless
      7. enjoyment   9. scientist
      8. heroism   10. context
      10. confront   12. progress
      11. helpless   13. fortieth
      14. antichrist   14. antidote
      15. foolish   15. fourth
      16. program
      17. eighth

2.90 a. addition
      b. celebration
      c. separation
      d. cautious
      e. relationship
      f. lonesome
      g. afterward
      h. burdensome
      i. fabulous
      j. authorship
      k. friendship
      l. quarrelsome
      m. homeward

2.91 a. halves
      b. thieves
      c. pianos
      d. heroes
      e. echoes
      f. solos
      g. beliefs

2.92 Teacher check

SECTION THREE

3.1   mythical story

3.2   Sweden

3.3   Example:
He was a mythical monster, half
man and half beast.

3.4   Example:
They lived in Denmark.

3.5   Fourteen men went with Beowulf
to the King.

3.6   Beowulf and his companions rested in
the hall to await Grendel's coming.

3.7   b

3.8   f

3.9   a

3.10 c

3.11 e

3.12 d

3.13 I. The Departure
    B. Father gives inheritance to son
  II.
    A. Famine comes to the land
  III. The Repentance
    C. Son is sorry for sins
  IV.
    A. Father runs and kisses son
    C. Father orders best robe,
      ring, and shoes for son

3.14 Example:
A son asks for an inheritance and goes
to a far country. Because of a wasted
inheritance and famine, he ends up
feeding swine. Remembering his
father's well-treated servants, he
repents and decides to return home.
His father greets him with a kiss.
He tells his father of his
unworthiness, but his father
orders the best robe, ring, and
shoes for his son.

3.15 Examples:
Mafatu's people worshipped courage,
but Esther's people worshipped God.
Mafatu was Polynesian and Esther
was Jewish. Mafatu was the son of
a great chief and Esther was a
queen. Mafatu had to face the
sea. Esther had to face the king.
Mafatu faced the sea alone, but
Esther had placed her life in
God's hands.

3.16 Examples:
Mafatu and Esther were both in
royal families. They both were
afraid of something. They both
were courageous.

3.17 trusting in the Lord

3.18 trust, delight, commit

3.19 do good

3.20 the desires of my heart

3.21 my way

3.22 1. cause me to dwell in the land
    and feed on His faithfulness
  2. give me the desires of my heart
  3. bring it to pass

3.23 Example:
the fact that God wants me to
delight in Him and He will give
me the desires of my heart

3.24 a. (.) request
  b. (?) question
  c. (!) exclamation
  d. (.) command
  e. (.) statement

3.25 CS

3.26 fragment

3.27 CS

3.28 CS

3.29 fragment

3.30 P

3.31 P

3.32 S

3.33 P

SECTION THREE (cont.)

3.34 S

3.35 John rode his bicycle to the store.

3.36 The girl with a hat bought a plant.

3.37 A bird is nesting in the tree.

3.38 The lion with a hurt paw
befriended the man. <u>or</u>
The man befriended the lion
with a hurt paw.

3.39 Example:
The little, wooden puppet sat on
the old dresser.

3.40 Example:
The little child sat sadly in his yard.

3.41 taught

3.42 Teacher check

3.43 Teacher check

3.44 a. cite, sight
b. idle, idol
c. miner, minor

3.45 a. ch
b. cious
c. sion
d. tion
e. ss
f. s

3.46 Either order:
a. fought
b. caught

3.47 a. shriek
b. tough, drought
c. rhythm
d. brief
e. conquer

3.48 a. weigh, way
b. waste, waist

3.49 a. pet
b. dopt
c. cal
d. ban
e. ap
f. count
g. mate
h. place

3.50 Any order:
a. fatal
b. nickel
c. bottle

3.51 a. e
b. s
c. gh

3.52 a. feat, feet
b. peace, piece
c. steal, steel

3.53 Teacher check

SELF TEST 1

1.01 Any order:
   a. reading
   b. listening
   c. speaking
   d. writing
1.02 e
1.03 a
1.04 d
1.05 c
1.06 h
1.07 j
1.08 f
1.09 i
1.010 b
1.011 g
1.012 a   style
   b. topic
1.013 noun
1.014 dialogue
1.015 a. Underline
   b. List
   c. Write
1.016 Example:
   Titles usually contain the main
   idea of the paragraph or story.

1.017 true
1.018 false
1.019 false
1.020 true
1.021 true
1.022 A vowel sound can be spelled with
   one or more vowel letters. Vowels
   have more than one sound for each
   vowel letter.
1.023 a. Look at the word; pronounce it.
   b. Listen for all the sounds; spell
      the word out loud.
   c. Copy the word on paper and read
      each letter.
   d. Write the word without looking
      at it.
      Check the spelling and correct.
   e. Practice writing the word in
      sentences.
1.024 Any order:
   a. oi;   Example: coil
   b. oy;   Example: coy
   c. ou;   Example: couch
   d. ow;   Example: crowd

SELF TEST 2

2.01 e
2.02 a
2.03 a
2.04 d
2.05 c
2.06 b
2.07 Flying to New York
2.08 Flying over Mediterranean Sea
2.09 Going to Nazareth on donkey
2.010 Dr. Martin begins talking about Jesus
2.011 Students asking questions
2.012 Any order:

   a. how many syllables a word has
   b. how vowels are pronounced
      according to diacritical marks
   c. where the accent mark is placed
2.013 The entry word shows the correct
   spelling. The respelling is
   spelled to show the correct sounds
   and to help pronounce the word.
2.014 e
2.015 g
2.016 a
2.017 f

SELF TEST 2 (cont.)

2.018 b

2.019 c

2.020 d

2.021 diphthong

2.022 digraph

2.023 In order:

    a. Listen for all the sounds;
       spell the word orally.

    b. Copy the word.

    c. Write the word without copying;
       check the spelling.

2.024 a. creature or eastern

    b. ew

    c. roaster or loader

    d. ai

    e. sower or growing

    f. au

SELF TEST 3

3.01 Jesus is

3.02 ridiculed

3.03 skills

3.04 handwriting

3.05 silent

3.06 respellings

3.07 thy hand findeth to do, do it with thy might

3.08 Any order:

    space

    shape

    size

    stroke

    slant

3.09 a blend of two vowel sounds

3.010 one sound formed by two vowel letters

3.011 a word or part of a word with one vowel sound

3.012 a. What is happening in the story.

    b. Where the story is happening.

    c. Who the people are in the story.

3.013 In order:

    a. Look at the word and pronounce it.

    b. Copy the word on paper and read each letter.

    c. Write the word without looking at it, and check your spelling.

3.014 A good title will include the topic word. The topic word helps the reader to know the main idea of a paragraph.

3.015 Any order:

    a. reading

    b. listening

    c. speaking

    d. writing

3.016 Examples:

    a. coat

    b. chew

    c. eat

    d. train

    e. meet

    f. bay

3.017 Examples:

    vowel

    poison

    royal

    mountain

SELF TEST 1

1.01 Polynesia

1.02 chief

1.03 fishing

1.04 worshiped

1.05 violence

1.06 albatross

1.07 dog

1.08 outrigger

1.09 missionaries

1.010 barrier-reef

1.011-1.020 Examples:

1.011 someone

1.012 houseboat

1.013 ice cream

1.014 outrigger

1.015 bareback

1.016 blacksmith

1.017 grandmother

1.018 schoolyard

1.019 football

1.020 overboard

1.021 Examples:
have background experience
agree with other sources
agree with himself throughout
the selection

1.022 fact

1.023 opinion

1.024 Examples:
a. forever
b. ice cream
c. barrier-reef

1.025 Examples:
a. twenty-five
b. brand-new
c. go-ing

1.026 Example:
illustration

1.027 Example:
He may have taken Kana's out-rigger. Kana was his closest friend. Kana had talked to him about going with the boys. He would want Kana to know he had gone out to sea.

SELF TEST 2

2.01 courage

2.02 ideas

2.03 details

2.04 nouns

2.05 subject

2.06 adjectives

2.07 introductory

2.08 detail

2.09 summary

2.010 e

2.011 h

2.012 f

2.013 i

2.014 b

2.015 d

2.016 j

2.017 a

2.018 k

2.019 l

2.020 c

	Noun	Adjective
2.021	woman	
2.022		fluffy
2.023		powerful
2.024		lonely

SELF TEST 2 (cont.)

2.025 sea urchin

2.026 canoe

2.027 storm

2.028   old

2.029   pitiful

2.030   cranky

2.031 Example:

Mafatu was a Polynesian boy who was afraid of the sea. When he was three years old, he and his mother were in a hurricane. His mother died. Whenever Mafatu thought about this experience, he became very fearful. His fear was so great that it caused ill-luck when he went on a fishing voyage. Mafatu experienced resentment and hatred when he was left out by the other men and boys. His father was shamed by Mafatu's anxious fear. After hearing his best friend call him a coward, Mafatu and his companion, Uri, went out to face the sea alone.

SELF TEST 3

3.01 mood

3.02 think

3.03 fear

3.04 coward

3.05 two

3.06 nouns

3.07 adjectives

3.08 subject

3.09 h

3.010 f

3.011 g

3.012 c

3.013 i

3.014 a

3.015 b

3.016 e

3.017 j

3.018   a. noun

       b. adjective

       c. adjective

       d. verb

       e. verb

       f. verb

       g. noun

       h. noun

       i. noun

       j. noun

       k. verb

       l. verb

       m. verb

       n. adjective

       o. adjective

       p. noun

3.019 Poems should follow the diamante pattern and display change of mood or attitude as described in Answer Key 3.11

3.020 true

3.021 false

3.022 true

3.023 true

3.024 true

3.025 true

SELF TEST 1

1.01

1.02   s

1.03   s

1.05   s

1.06   s

1.08   s

1.09   s

1.011   3

1.012   1

1.013   5

1.014   2

1.015   4

1.016   <u>People the world over</u> <u>need</u> <u>salvation</u>.

1.017   <u>Bill and his friends</u> <u>attend</u> <u>church</u>.

1.018   <u>God</u> <u>sent His only begotten Son</u>.

1.019   <u>wĭnd</u>

1.020   <u>bou</u>

1.021   pasteurize

1.022   Louis Pasteur

1.023   by heating the milk

1.024   raw milk

1.025   by performing a famous deed

1.026   when it has been pasteurized

1.027   Example:
        One way of creating a new word is
        by performing a famous deed.

1.028   act of making something

1.029   a helper; a husband or wife

1.030   something that comes before

1.031   having no like or equal

1.032   Language was first used in the garden
        of Eden when man named the animals.

SELF TEST 2

2.01 The, disgusted, slowly, the

2.02 often, the, the, the, towering

2.03 The, modest, meekly, the

2.04 The, efficiently, the, intelligent

2.05 That, ancient, not, well

2.06 s

2.09 s

2.010 s

2.011 The boy in the back seat
was jumping up and down.

2.012 Everyone in town went to the
parade.

2.013 We had fun at the zoo.

2.014 Our radio and our record player
are not working.

2.015 Have you studied for the test?

2.016 un

2.017 in

2.018 im

2.019 in

2.020 un

2.021 less

2.022 ful

2.023 ful

2.024 able

2.025 less

2.026 Adam and Eve became sinners when
they ate from the tree of the
knowledge of good and evil.

2.027 Cain became very jealous when he
saw that God accepted Abel's offering.

2.028 Denying our sins
keeps us from God's forgiveness.

2.029 Lucifer wanted to overthrow God, so
he was cast out of heaven.

2.030 Cain was not forgiven of his sin
because he refused to ask God to
forgive him.

2.031 Our product will keep your family
healthy and free from danger.

2.032 Our product is better than all the other
products.

2.033 Our product is not as expensive as the
other products.

2.034 You need this product to help you have
everything your neighbors have.

SELF TEST 3

3.01	d		3.023	able
3.02	a		3.024	ful
3.03	g		3.025	able
3.04	e		3.026	a nervous feeling
3.05	j		3.027	waste your money
3.06	b		3.028	makes a great effort
3.07	h		3.029	was no longer controlled
3.08	i		3.030	very large
3.09	f		3.031	Most mystery stories are written to entertain.
3.010	c		3.032	Example:
3.011	wind			God's purpose in having men write
3.012	wīnd			the Bible was to instruct man,
3.013	rēd			to give man directions, to guide
3.014	red			people's lives, to present the
3.015	un			plan of salvation.
3.016	in			
3.017	im			
3.018	un			
3.019	im			
3.020	in			
3.021	ful			
3.022	less			

SELF TEST 1

1.01	environmental
1.02	Either one:
	geologist
	or geochemist
1.03	particles
1.04	exhaust
1.05	analyzed
1.06	lead
1.07	accumulative
1.08	microscopic
1.09	industrial
1.010	especially
1.011	fact
1.012	opinion
1.013	fact
1.014	fact
1.015	opinion
1.016	fertilizes the flower by carrying pollen from blossom to blossom
1.017	carries the pollen from one head of wheat to another
1.018	use reference books
1.019	bought his ticket and checked his luggage
1.020	bell rang and children laughingly walked out the door
1.021-1.024	Any order:

1.021	statement
1.022	request - command
1.023	question
1.024	exclamation
1.025-1.028	Any order:
1.025	statement - period
1.026	request - command - period
1.027	question - question mark
1.028	exclamation - exclamation point
1.029-1.033	Any order:
1.029	space
1.030	shape
1.031	size
1.032	stroke
1.033	slant
1.034	a. syllables
	b. vowel
1.035	vowel digraph
1.036	ea
1.037	ea
1.038	oa
1.039	ee
1.040	ee
1.041	ai
1.042	au
1.043	au
1.044	ow
1.045	ow

SELF TEST 2

2.01	thought
2.02	God
2.03	structure
2.04	two
2.05	subject
2.06	predicate
2.07	adjectives
2.08	adverbs
2.09	Any two of the three: adjectives, signal words, or noun signals

2.010	nouns
2.011	kind
2.012	many
2.013	one
2.014-2.016	Any order:
2.014	how
2.015	where
2.016	when
2.017	adverbs
2.018	adverb
2.019	adjective

2.020	capital	2.035	S
2.021	true	2.036-2.038	Any order:
2.022	true	2.036	slant
2.023	false	2.037	stroke
2.024	false	2.038	size
2.025	true	2.039	space
2.026	true	2.040	shape
2.027	true	2.041	a. gh
2.028	false		b. f
2.029	false		c. ph
2.030	false	2.042	d. n
2.031	S		e. k, e
2.032	M	2.043	h. c
2.033	M		i. c, e
2.034	M		j. t

SELF TEST 3

3.01	A red striped beach umbrella	3.025-3.028	Any order:
3.02	Mark	3.025	select a topic
3.03	My book	3.026	gather information
3.04	The whole class	3.027	make an outline
3.05	Zack and Marty	3.028	write the report
3.06	liked all of his morning classes	3.029	first
3.07	forgot to stow the supplies properly	3.030	first
3.08	planned a surprise party for their teacher	3.031	second
		3.032	third
3.09	went to Mexico for his vacation	3.033	Example:
3.010	are good companions		The outline is your guide for writing. The main ideas of an outline can be used as introductory sentences for each paragraph. The sub-topics and details are supporting detail sentences in the paragraphs.
3.011	true		
3.012	false		
3.013	false		
3.014	true		
3.015	false	3.034	f
3.016	true	3.035	j
3.017	false	3.036	b
3.018	false	3.037	i
3.019	true	3.038	k
3.020	true	3.039	e
3.021	read	3.040	c
3.022	listen	3.041	g
3.023	observe	3.042	a
3.024	question	3.043	d

SELF TEST 1

1.01	true		1.024	good, clear language or pleasant language
1.02	false		1.025	effect
1.03	false		1.026	b
1.04	false		1.027	a
1.05	true		1.028	b
1.06	false		1.029	b
1.07	false		1.030	c
1.08	true		1.031	a
1.09	false		1.032	c
1.010	true		1.033	a
1.011	a		1.034	a
1.012	k		1.035	b
1.013	b		1.036	Examples:
1.014	j			Arthur was willing to be helpful. He was truthful. He was loyal. He sometimes acted before he thought about things.
1.015	d			
1.016	i			
1.017	e			
1.018	h		1.037	Examples:
1.019	f			The people of Arthur's day believed in magic and magicians. They also thought it was not wrong to swear by the Bible.
1.020	g			
1.021	the kind of story told			
1.022	word pictures			
1.023	time in history			

SELF TEST 2

2.01	true
2.02	false
2.03	false
2.04	true
2.05	false
2.06	false
2.07	false
2.08	true
2.09	false
2.010	false
2.011	not biological brothers
2.012	one lie
2.013	acted without thinking
2.014	partly truth, partly imagination
2.015	father
2.016	helped him think it through
2.017	was supposed to be king
2.018	did not
2.019	talking it out
2.020	not enough
2.021	poor
2.022	poor
2.023	poor
2.024	good
2.025	good
2.026	poor
2.027	good
2.028	poor

2.029 poor

2.030 poor

2.031 "This hamburger is the greatest!" Jim exclaimed.

2.032 "Now, who spilled the paint?" Mother asked.

2.033 Said Bob, "I don't like the way this looks."

2.034 Susan said, "I was trying to surprise you."

2.035 "Stop right where you are!" shouted the policeman.

2.036 Example:
Having a bad knee, Tim found the hill too steep to climb.

2.037 Example:
Annette had a cold lunch of yesterday's leftovers and a glass of milk.

2.038 Example:
A story in Boy's Life interested me while I was waiting for the dentist.

2.039 Example:
After we had hiked all morning, our hunger was bigger than our lunches.

2.040 Example:
Belle looked great in her new dress, which was made of pink cotton.

SELF TEST 3

3.01	true	
3.02	true	
3.03	false	
3.04	true	
3.05	false	
3.06	true	
3.07	true	
3.08	true	
3.09	false	
3.010	false	
3.011	e	
3.012	b	
3.013	j	
3.014	d	
3.015	k	
3.016	c	
3.017	a	
3.018	f	
3.019	i	
3.020	h	
3.021	seed idea	
3.022	pictures	
3.023	a.	setting
	b.	characters
	c.	action
3.024	dialogue	
3.025	draft	

3.026 c. small children
3.027 a. subjects
3.028 a. past
3.029 b. descriptive
3.030 a. lively
3.031 c. noun
3.032 a. comma
3.033 b. quotation marks
3.034 b. want to read the story
3.035 a. come alive

3.036 Example:
A story can help me to be a better person if the story tells how someone solved a problem and I can learn to solve a problem like that.

3.037 Example:
If you keep a file of story materials, you will have seed ideas, pictures of people and the kind of clothing they wear, and pictures to describe for settings.

SELF TEST 1

1.01	false	1.029	might, months, years, days
1.02	false	1.030	wind, tor-, dark-
1.03	true	1.031	Meg, was, mar-
1.04	true	1.032	7
1.05	false	1.033	2
1.06	true	1.034	1
1.07	false	1.035	8
1.08	false	1.036	6
1.09	false	1.037	3
1.010	true	1.038	5
1.011	false	1.039	4

1.012 d

1.013 h

1.014 f

1.015 a

1.016 b

1.017 i

1.018 c

1.019 g

1.020 k

1.021 j

1.022 a

1.023 a

1.024 b

1.025 b

1.026 a

1.027 wak-, sleep-

1.028 bo-, hand, neck, spanned

1.040 Example:

The poet's purpose was to honor the Pilgrim Fathers for being brave enough to come to a difficult land in order to have freedom to worship God according to their faith.

1.041 Example:

He wanted to honor Barbara Frietchie for being patriotic and brave.

1.042 Any order:

a. rhythm

b. language

c. emotion

SELF TEST 2

2.01 true

2.02 false

2.03 true

2.04 false

2.05 true

2.06 false

2.07 true

2.08 true

2.09 false

2.010 true

2.011 b

2.012 b

2.013 c

2.014 a

2.015 c

2.016 a

2.017 c

2.018 a

2.019 c

2.020 a

2.021 a. unstressed

b. stressed

2.022 palindrome

2.023 five

2.024 puns

2.025 pictures

2.026 rhythm

2.027 conundrum

2.028 second

2.029 cadence

2.030 symbol

2.031 fort-, space, thee, give

2.032 home, Ab-, com-, cold

2.033 none, know, Lon-, town

2.034 was, girl, Cloud

2.035 she, pon-

2.036 can-, tas-, tooth-

2.037 Example:

The idea taught by this poem was that humor can sometimes get you out of difficulty.

2.038 Example:

The poet told that different people came to find freedom to worship God according to their faith, even though the trip was difficult and the place they came to was a wild place.

2.039 Example:

Barbara Frietchie's hanging out the flag (and/or her cry to General Jackson) was a symbol of loyalty (or patriotism). General Jackson's telling his soldiers to leave the flag alone was a symbol of respect.

SELF TEST 3

3.01 false

3.02 false

3.03 true

3.04 true

3.05 false

3.06 false

3.07 true

3.08 false

3.09 true

3.010 true

3.011 d

3.012 h

3.013 j

3.014 i

3.015 a

3.016 b

3.017 g

3.018 c

3.019 k

3.020 f

3.021 most

3.022 quatrain

3.023 limerick

3.024 palindrome

3.025 conundrum

3.026 emphasis or stress

3.027 puns

3.028 inspirational

3.029 economize

3.030 words

3.031 a

3.032 b

3.033 a

3.034 Who's, -fraid, big, wolf

3.035 Hick-, dick-, dock, mouse, up, clock

3.036 all, up, at-, play

3.037 Example:

The poem shows the blacksmith as an honest, hard-working man who loved his family and God.

3.038 Example:

When people are lonely, they may try to draw attention to themselves so someone will notice them.

3.039 Any order:

a. rhythm

b. language

c. emotion

SELF TEST 1

1.01 She was swimming all day.

1.02 She got a bad sunburn.

1.03 The lightning caused the fire.

1.04 It started a forest fire.

1.05 The zookeeper left the gate unlocked.

1.06 The lion got loose.

1.07 famished

1.08 shrill

1.09 complexion

1.010 ointment

1.011 transparent

1.012 mingle

1.013 perceived

1.014 wrench

1.015 voyage

1.016 potion

1.017 2

1.018 4

1.019 1

1.020 5

1.021 3

1.022 8

1.023 7

1.024 6

1.025 b. six inches tall.

1.026 a. a cart with twenty-two wheels.

1.027 c. temple ruin.

1.028 a. green with forests and fields.

1.029 c. took care of Gulliver.

1.030 a. two men.

1.031 b. drilled on top of Gulliver's handkerchief.

1.032 c. was set free.

1.033 Teacher check

1.034 Teacher check

1.035 Teacher check

1.036 Teacher check

1.037 Teacher check

1.038 Teacher check

SELF TEST 2

2.01 The roads were icy and there was a sharp turn.

2.02 He slid off the road.

2.03 voyage

2.04 famished

2.05 mingle

2.06 shrill

2.07 wrench

2.08 parachute

2.09 scout

2.010 salad

2.011 Rebekah

2.012 France

2.013 Lincoln Memorial

2.014 valleys

2.015 children

2.016 lizards

2.017 babies

2.018 teachers'

2.019 shepherd's

2.020 oxen's

2.021 rabbits, (carrot)

2.022 girl (song)

2.023 man, (book)

2.024 She

2.025 them

2.026 We

2.027-2.029 Examples:

2.027 their

2.028 his

2.029 its

2.030-2.034 Examples:

2.030 The teachers' meeting was on Friday.

2.031 Their meeting was on Friday.

2.032 The Pacific Ocean is large.

2.033 The men's team won the game.

2.034 Their team won the game.

SELF TEST 3

3.01   Bugs were in the new house.
3.02   By the end of the week, there were no more bugs.
3.03   ointment
3.04   debate
3.05   embroider
3.06   inhabitants
3.07   perceived
3.08   Jeff, (store)
3.09   turkeys
3.010   children's
3.011   boy, (bicycle)
3.012   a. She
        b. her
3.013   b. Be careful with fire in the forest.
3.014   wrong
3.015   right
3.016   Jane and her father did not catch any fish.
3.017   O
3.018   F
3.019   O
3.020   F

3.021   c. embarrassment
3.022   a. excitement
3.023   purge
3.024   distress
3.025   martyr
3.026   refuge
3.027   c. the "cave people"
3.028   a. brother died in prison
3.029   b. in prison
3.030   c. forgave Paul
3.031   Teacher check
3.032   Teacher check

SELF TEST 4

4.01-4.08 Examples:

4.01 hungry

4.02 a. small

b. little

4.03 new

4.04 good

4.05 a. little

b. brown

4.06 Three

4.07 many

4.08 Some

4.09 The friendly dolphins jumped into the blue water.

4.010 The cold floor was filthy and the bare walls were ugly.

4.011-4.012 Examples:

4.011 The noisy cricket sat on the huge fireplace.

4.012 A tall, skinny, dirty boy ran to the big grocery store.

4.013 famished

4.014 refuge

4.015 shrill

4.016 debate

4.017 inhabitants

4.018 mingled

4.019 persecution

4.020 martyr

4.021 The tall, strange visitor quickly jumped the high rail fence.

4.022 The busy cave people saw two young men coming.

4.023 Teacher check

4.024 The dogs ate the dog food.

4.025 They were hungry.

4.026 Tom went to get their dog food.

4.027 Possessive

baby's

carrot's

man's

teacher's

Plural

babies

carrots

men

teachers

SELF TEST 1

1.01 <u>were</u> <u>jogging</u>

1.02 <u>called</u>

1.03 <u>traveled</u>

1.04 <u>won</u>

1.05 <u>will</u> <u>go</u>

1.06 <u>was</u> <u>raining</u>

1.07 <u>were</u> <u>barking</u>

1.08 <u>will be</u> <u>playing</u>

1.09 <u>practice</u>

1.010 <u>practices</u>

1.011 regular

1.012 irregular

1.013 irregular

1.014 regular

1.015 irregular

1.016 irregular

1.017 irregular

1.018 regular

1.019 regular

1.020 regular

1.021 <u>are</u>, being

1.022 <u>followed</u>, action

1.023 <u>was</u>, being

1.024 <u>will jump</u>, action

1.025 <u>will be</u>, being

1.026 aren't

1.027 hasn't

1.028 I'm

1.029 He's

1.030 They're

1.031 d

1.032 e

1.033 b

1.034 a

1.035 b

1.036 Example:

God has no beginning or ending.

He is!

1.037 Example:

The verb tells what the subject

is or what the subject is doing.

SELF TEST 2

2.01   false

2.02   false

2.03   true

2.04   true

2.05   false

2.06   true

2.07   true

2.08   true

2.09   true

2.010   true

2.011   Example:

You can't please everyone.

2.012   Example:

The farmer could not make up his
mind and stay with his decision.

2.013   India

2.014   To teach a moral
or to teach a lesson.

2.015   Example:

It means that the reader will know
what the moral is without being
told specifically.

2.016   7

2.017   3

2.018   5

2.019   6

2.020   10

2.021   1

2.022   9

2.023   4

2.024   2

2.025   8

2.026   laziness

2.027   according to the rule

2.028   get off of an animal

2.029   not a true story; imaginary

2.030   meet unexpectedly

2.031   irregular

2.032   regular

2.033   regular

2.034   irregular

2.035   regular

2.036   regular

2.037   irregular

2.038   irregular

2.039   regular

2.040   regular

2.041   he's

2.042   they've

2.043   isn't

2.044   we're

2.045   they're

2.046   Example:

Jesus told parables because people like
to listen to stories and He could teach
them lessons through the stories.

SELF TEST 3

3.01 <u>swinging</u>
3.02 <u>Howling</u>
3.03 <u>snoring</u>
3.04 <u>trading</u>
3.05 <u>Singing</u>
3.06 <u>are</u>
3.07 <u>is</u>
3.08 <u>were</u>
3.09 A parable is a story about people, used to illustrate a spiritual meaning. A fable is an imaginary story, often with talking animals, used to picture a moral lesson.
3.010 Its secret message must be revealed by God.
3.011 P <u>were</u>
3.012 S <u>is</u>
3.013 S <u>was</u>
3.014 P <u>were</u>
3.015 P
3.016 F
3.017 P
3.018 P
3.019 P
3.020 F
3.021 P
3.022 F
3.023 F
3.024 P

3.025 false
3.026 false
3.027 true
3.028 true
3.029 true
3.030 true
3.031 true
3.032 true
3.033 false
3.034 graciously
3.035 lovingly
3.036 thoughtfully
3.037 a. comparison of two things
        b. comparison of more than two things
3.038 clerical
3.039 electrical
3.040 financial
3.041 Racial
3.042 spiritual

SELF TEST 1

1.01	b	1.024	c
1.02	d	1.025	b
1.03	c	1.026	a
1.04	a	1.027	b
1.05	c	1.028	a
1.06	b	1.029	b
1.07	d	1.030	b
1.08	a	1.031	b
1.09	Read slowly for details	1.032	a
1.010	Scan	1.033	miracle of Jesus
1.011	Skim	1.034	John 6:15 through 21
1.012	Scan	1.035	They left by ship.
1.013	Read slowly for details	1.036	Capernaum
1.014	Skim	1.037	"It is I; be not afraid."
1.015	Scan	1.038	c
1.016	Skim	1.039	a
1.017	scientific discovery	1.040	b
1.018	Marie and Pierre Curie	1.041	a
1.019	November 7, 1869	1.042	c
1.020	Poland	1.043	b
1.021	a physicist	1.044	a
1.022	1891	1.045	b
1.023	Sorbonne		

SELF TEST 2

2.01	c	2.028	Solomon's Temple
2.02	a	2.029	150,000
2.03	d	2.030	seven years
2.04	b	2.031	a
2.05	e	2.032	b
2.06	a	2.033	b
2.07	c	2.034	c
2.08	a	2.035	a
2.09	d	2.036	c
2.010	b	2.037	seven
2.011	fossils	2.038	Holy of Holies
2.012	plant and animal	2.039	Thirty thousand men to cut timber
2.013	rocks	2.040	The Completed Temple
2.014	a	2.041	Stone walls lined with carved cedar
2.015	c	2.042	Inside covered with pure gold
2.016	a		
2.017	b		
2.018	a fish		
2.019	A plant impression left on a stone		
2.020	An animal impression left in stone		
2.021	How are Fossils Made?		
2.022	Plants or animals fell in soft clay a long time ago		
2.023	The clay turned to rock		
2.024	c		
2.025	b		
2.026	e		
2.027	a		

SELF TEST 3

3.01   fc

3.02   b

3.03   e

3.04   c

3.05   g

3.06   a

3.07   a missionary journey

3.08   Paul

3.09   Turkey

3.010   Barnabas and John Mark

3.011   a

3.012   c

3.013   b

3.014   a

3.015   c

3.016   b

3.017   two lakes

3.018   twice

3.019   The Journey

3.020   Return trip began in Derbe, back through Lystra, Iconium, Pisidian Antioch, then to Attalia, and by ship to Antioch

3.021   Reception of the Missionaries

3.022   Many received Jesus Christ

3.023   People in Iconium plotted to stone them

3.024   Paul stoned by rocks at Lystra

3.025   b

3.026   d

3.027   a

3.028   e

3.029   f

3.030   O

3.031   F

3.032   F

3.033   O

3.034   Example:

My school is called Grace Academy.

3.035   Example:

My school is the best in town.

3.036   the body of writings of a period, language, or country, especially those writings kept alive by their beauty or effectiveness of style or thought.

3.037   c

3.038   b

3.039   a

3.040   b

3.041   a

3.042   c

3.043   a

SELF TEST 1

1.01	true
1.02	false
1.03	false
1.04	true
1.05	true
1.06	false
1.07	true
1.08	true
1.09	false
1.010	true
1.011	b
1.012	f
1.013	c
1.014	a
1.015	h
1.016	j
1.017	i
1.018	e
1.019	g
1.020	d
1.021	b. suspense
1.022	a. only a few characters
1.023	c. novel
1.024	a. parable
1.025	b. cadence
1.026	a. imitation of sounds
1.027	c. repetition of sounds
1.028	c. poetic form
1.029	a. inspirational poems
1.030	b. limerick
1.031	PN England
1.032	CN professor

1.033 papers
1.034 ladies
1.035 children
1.036 pastors'
1.037 aunt's
1.038 sheep's
1.039 The young <u>man</u> / wrote a (story.)
1.040 The <u>shepherds</u> / grazed their (sheep.)
1.041 them
1.042 He
1.043 its
1.044 her
1.045 Example:
The bright, golden sun came up over the snow-capped mountains.
1.046 Example; any order:
a. Is the story told in good, clear language?
b. Does the language match the kind of story it told?
c. Does the language give you a feeling for the time of history in which the story takes place?
or Is the language pleasant to read? Does the language paint word pictures in your mind? Do the characters seem to talk the way people of their age and time in history would?

SELF TEST 2

2.01	false	2.030	b. syllables and pronunciations
2.02	true	2.031	IR
2.03	false	2.032	R
2.04	false	2.033	R
2.05	true	2.034	IR
2.06	true	2.035	are or were
2.07	false	2.036	is or was
2.08	true	2.037	teacher's
2.09	false	2.038	school's
2.010	true	2.039	ran
2.011	c	2.040	quickly
2.012	k	2.041	young
2.013	d	2.042	very
2.014	a	2.043	home
2.015	f	2.044	George
2.016	j	2.045	is
2.017	b	2.046	going
2.018	h	2.047	radiantly
2.019	g	2.048	she
2.020	e	2.049	never
2.021	a. purpose	2.050	its
2.022	c. plot	2.051	faster
2.023	b. decide what probably happened	2.052	raging
2.024	c. heteronyms	2.053	past, present, future
2.025	b. simile	2.054	Example:
2.026	a. symbolism		Mary will sit on this chair.
2.027	c. legend		future
2.028	a. stanzas		
2.029	b. fable		

SELF TEST 3

3.01	true	3.033	sleeping
3.02	false	3.034	bed
3.03	true	3.035	John
3.04	true	3.036	soft
3.05	false	3.037	is
3.06	false	3.038	its
3.07	true	3.039	?
3.08	true	3.040	.
3.09	false	3.041	!
3.010	false	3.042	CS
3.011	d	3.043	N
3.012	e	3.044	CS
3.013	h	3.045	N
3.014	j	3.046	The healed man leaped for joy.
3.015	c	3.047	"I'm going to the store now," Mother said. Bob replied, "May I go with you?"
3.016	k		
3.017	b		
3.018	f		
3.019	i		
3.020	a		
3.021	b. outlining		
3.022	a. graphic aids		
3.023	a. summarizing		
3.024	c. predicate part		
3.025	b. reaction		
3.026	c. drama		
3.027	b. Christian judgments		
3.028	a. implied meaning		
3.029	c. ballad		
3.030	c. opinion		
3.031	lay		
3.032	quietly		

Notes

1. c

2. d

3. e

4. a

5. h

6. g

7. b

8. f

9. Any order:
Noting important details
Classifying information
Making predictions
Recognizing accuracy and
thoughtfulness
Developing a vocabulary
Developing a good attitude

10. syllable

11. digraph

12. diphthong

13. silent

14. dialogue

15. Any order:
space
shape
size
stroke
slant

16. topic

17. Examples:
a. ou; account
b. ow; vowel
c. oi; jointly
d. oy; voyage

18. Any four; any order:
a. ea; read
b. ew; fewer
c. ai; failure
d. au; saucer
e. ay; bay
f. oo; book
g. ee; meet
h. oa; coat

19. e

20. g

21. a

22. d

23. h

24. b

25. j

26. c

27. f

28. i

1. courage

2. fear

3. coward

4. mood

5. details

6. subject

7. nouns

8. adjectives

9. two

10. verbs

11. Example: schoolhouse

12. Example: ice cream

13. Example: barrier-reef

14. Example: twenty-five

15. Example: one-of-a-kind

16. Example: discus-sion

17. Example: dog

18. Example: nondescript

19. Example: looking

20. Example: doctor

21. Example: resentment

22. Example: can't

23. Example:
     Mafatu was the son of the
     island chief.

24. Example:
     Mafatu took Kana's outrigger
     canoe.

25. Paragraphs will vary; teacher check
     Score 5 points for using sentences.
     Score 3 points for handwriting.
     Score 3 points for correct spelling.
     Score 3 points for using adjectives
     and interesting details.

26. d

27. f

28. h

29. a

30. b

31. i

32. c

33. e

34. j

35. k

36. l

1. true

2. false

3. false

4. true

5. true

6. true

7. true

8. false

9. true

10. false

11. 2

12. 5

13. 3

14. 1

15. 4

16. ri kôrd'

17. mĭ nut'

18. this is not a complete sentence
19. s
20. s

21. The Bible record proves that God used language.
22. The power and ability to communicate is a divine characteristic.

23. The boy was injured when he fell from his bicycle.
24. Due to carelessness, the car was not repaired correctly.
25. The ice melted when we forgot to put it in the freezer.
26. ful or less

27. in

28. un

29. able

30. im

31. The, enormous, wildly

32. swiftly, the, the, sleek, a

33. A, refreshing, often

34. d

35. b

36. a

37. c

38. gave me a ride

39. told a story
40. God told Adam to name the animals. Language was a gift of God.
41. Our product will keep your family healthy and free from danger.

1. The happy, excited boys had seen the life cycle of a moth.
2. c. summary
3. 1
4. 3
5. 2
6. 4
7. opinion
8. question
9. request or command
10. exclamation
11. five S's of handwriting
12. statement of fact
13. statement
14. a roaring lion
15. like cotton pillows on a blue sheet
16. X
17.
18.
19. X
20. X
21.
22. X
23.
24. X
25. X
26. a
27. e
28. f
29. b

30. g
31. i
32. c
33. d
34. Good for the health
35.-36. Either order:
35. Welcome change from the heat
36. Invigorating air
37. Good for fall sports
38.-40. Any order:
38. Football
39. Soccer
40. Hiking
41. adj.
42. adv.
43. adj.
44. adv.
45. adv.
46. Examples:
   Robin Hood wanted to be an honest forester. The foresters were dishonest. Robin Hood helped people. The foresters treated people badly. Robin Hood was tricked. The foresters tricked people.
47. selecting a topic
48. gathering information
49. outlining information
50. writing from the outline

1. Anyway
2. fewer
3. Let
4. accept

5. well

6. true

7. true

8. false

9. true
10. false

11. true

12. true
13. true

14. false
15. false

16. c
17. f

18. k
19. a
20. i
21. j
22. g

23. e
24. h
25. b
26. a. Was the story told in good, clear language?
    b. Did the language match the kind of story it told?
    c. Did the language give you a feeling for the time in history?
    d. Was the language pleasant to read?
    or Did the language paint word pictures in your mind?
    Did the characters seem to talk as people of their age and time in history would?
27. Any order:
    a. the kinds of words
    b. the action
    c. the suspense
28. Any order:
    a. setting
    b. characters
    c. action
29. a. 2
    b. 4
    c. 3
    d. 5
    e. 1
30. cross old lady
31. mother
32. tough kid
33. kind old lady
34. baby brother

1.	true	21.	rhythm
2.	false	22.	read aloud
3.	true	23.	ballads
4.	true	24.	fifth
5.	false	25.	forms
6.	true	26.	devices
7.	true	27.	better
8.	true	28.	economize
9.	false	29.	riddle
10.	false	30.	metaphor
11.	e	31.	MP
12.	g	32.	MP
13.	c	33.	LP
14.	i	34.	MP
15.	h	35.	MP
16.	a	36.	By, crag-, hill-, through, moss-, there
17.	b	37.	mer-, mer-, up, air
18.	k	38.	Up, jump, morn-, ear-
19.	d	39.	saw, lit-, ti-, Child, wait-, in, snow
20.	j	40.	fol-, lead-, one, one

1.	2	27.	feet
2.	1	28.	i
3.	3	29.	h
4.	2	30.	a
5.	3	31.	c
6.	4	32.	f
7.	1	33.	g
8.	c. Marc learned to forgive.	34.	j
9.	a. Kristi sent a card to a sick friend.	35.	b
10.	c. frightened	36.	e
11.	b. peaceful	37.	a. Mary forgot to water the plant.
			b. The plant died.
12.	true	38.	The small, brown mouse ran into the tiny hole.
13.	true		
14.	false	39.	Example:
			The bright fire burned in the dark night.
15.	true		
16.	false	40.	Karen fed the baby.
17.	true	41.	e
18.	false	42.	b
19.	false	43.	c
20.	true	44.	a
21.	true	45.	d
22.	mice	46.	f
23.	children	47.	d
24.	artists	48.	a
25.	toys	49.	f
26.	babies		

1. regular
2. irregular
3. helping
4. action
5. contraction
6. singular
7. adjective
8. tense
9. predicate
10. plural
11. <u>found</u>
12. <u>lived</u>
13. <u>made</u>
14. <u>are</u>
15. <u>escaped</u>
16. regular
17. irregular
18. irregular
19. irregular
20. regular
21. regular
22. regular
23. irregular
24. irregular
25. regular
26. (jumped) quickly
27. gladly, (helped)

28. (worked) better
29. badly (bruised)
30. very (hastily) (walked) off.
31. good
32. well
33. rapidly
34. are
35. brought
36. more rapidly
37. gave
38. sang
39. beautifully
40. quickly
41. an imaginary story
42. animals who can talk
43. teach a moral lesson
44. a story based on human situations
45. to teach a spiritual lesson

1.	c	28.	F
2.	b	29.	O
3.	a	30.	true
4.	i	31.	true
5.	e	32.	false
6.	h	33.	true
7.	d	34.	true
8.	k	35.	false
9.	j	36.	true
10.	f	37.	false
11.	protected bears	38.	false
12.	black and white	39.	e
13.	two feet long	40.	i
14.	a	41.	c
15.	b	42.	a
16.	a	43.	b
17.	c	44.	h
18.	c	45.	d
19.	Live in mountains of China	46.	g
20.	Eat bamboo		
21.	Koala Bears		
22.	Not really bears		
23.	Eat eucalyptus leaves		
24.	Protected by Australia		
25.	F		
26.	O		
27.	F		

1. true
2. true
3. true
4. true
5. false
6. true
7. false
8. true
9. false
10. false
11. b
12. e
13. h
14. a
15. f
16. i
17. d
18. k
19. j
20. c
21. b. judging a story's literary value
22. a. fiction and nonfiction
23. b. parable
24. c. symbolism
25. b. main idea
26. a. an idiom
27. b. heteronym
28. c. diagram
29. a. time line
30. c. speculating about events
31. The boy in the car saw the dolphin.
32. "Will you be in school tomorrow?" asked the teacher. Jeff replied, "No, I'm going on vacation."
33. CS
34. N
35. truck's
36. dogs'
37. The leaves on the trees are changing color.
38. falling
39. Rocky Mountains
40. snow
41. covered
42. black
43. is
44. violently
45. moving
46. never
47. its
48. majestically

ALTERNATE LIFEPAC TEST, Answer Key

1. g
2. i
3. h
4. f
5. b
6. c
7. d
8. a
9. silent
10. dialogue
11. diacritical
12. dictionary
13 plot
14. order
15. opinion
16. noun

17. Examples; any order:
    a. oi   oil
    b. oy   toy
    c. ow   cow
    d. ou   ouch
18. Examples; any order:
    a. ea   heat
    b. ew   chew
    c. oo   book
    d. ee   meet
19. h
20. i
21. g
22. a
23. j
24. f
25. e
26. c
27. d
28. b

1. language arts
2. courage
3. sea
4. mood
5. hyphen
6. main idea
7. adverbs
8. summarize
9. topic
10. adjectives
11.-22. Examples:
11. anger
12. house
13. sweetly
14. isn't
15. long-drawn
16. forty-two
17. headache
18. tidal wave
19. talk
20. walking
21. butter
22. minute
23. Example:
The early Polynesians worshiped courage.
24. Example:
Mafatu is a coward.

25. true
26. false
27. true
28. true
29. false
30. true
31. true
32. d
33. h
34. k
35. g
36. a
37. j
38. i
39. c
40. b
41. f

1. true
2. false
3. false
4. true
5. false
6. true
7. true
8. false
9. false
10. true
11. 5
12. 1
13. 4
14. 2
15. 3
16. wind
17. bou
18. S
19. NS
20. S
21. <u>The two boys explored the cave</u>.
22. <u>The rare butterfly was caught in the net</u>.
23. <u>The boy stayed out in the sun too long</u> and <u>received a severe sunburn</u>.
24. <u>A person can die</u> from <u>an inadequate supply of water</u>.
25. <u>With Jesus Christ in your life</u>, <u>you can have an abundant life</u>.
26. Example: (un)common
27. Example: joy(ful)
28. Example: pain(less)
29. Example: comfort(able)
30. Example: (im)perfect
31. <u>The</u> <u>pleasant</u> gentleman spoke <u>kindly</u> to <u>the</u> boy.
32. <u>The</u> <u>angry</u> grocer <u>quickly</u> added up <u>the</u> purchase.
33. <u>The</u> couple ate <u>often</u> in <u>the</u> <u>little</u> cafe.
34. b
35. d
36. a
37. c
38. in trouble
39. not controlled
40. Example: At the tower of Babel, God confused the people by creating different languages because they had gotten too proud. Since then, languages have changed and combined.
41. Example: Our product is better than all other products.

1. true
2. false
3. true
4. false
5. false
6. true
7. false
8. true
9. true
10. true
11. c.
12. Example:
    Years ago, people had not heard of fire engines.
13. 2
14. 5
15. 1
16. 3
17. 4
18. Putting out fires years ago
19. People yelled "Fire!" or rang church bells
20. A bucket brigade was formed
21. Putting out fires today
22. Fire trucks hook up to fire hydrants
23. F
24. O
25. O
26. F
27. a. E   b. !
28. a. S   b. .
29. a. Q   b. ?
30. a. RC   b. .

31. <u>The horses</u> <u>were harnessed to the plow.</u>
32. <u>The distant smoke signals</u> <u>relayed a message of trouble.</u>
33. ADJ
34. ADV
35. ADJ
36. ADV
37. S
38. S
39. M
40. M
41. Example:
    Cain and Abel were brothers. Cain was born first. Abel was a keeper of sheep and Cain was a tiller of the ground. Both brought an offering to the Lord, but Cain brought fruit and Abel brought a lamb. The Lord accepted Abel's offering but not Cain's. Cain was angry but Abel was not. Cain killed his brother.

1.	true	26.	i
2.	true	27.	j
3.	false	28.	l
4.	true	29.	Examples; any order:

29. Examples; any order:
   a. Did the language match the kind of story it told?
   b. Was the language pleasant to read?
   c. Did the language paint word pictures in your mind?
   d. Did the language give you a feeling for the time of history?
   or Was the story told in good clear language?
   or Did the characters seem to talk as people of their age and time in history would?

5.	false
6.	true
7.	true
8.	false
9.	false
10.	true
11.	P
12.	P
13.	G
14.	G
15.	characters
16.	setting
17.	action
18.	b
19.	f
20.	k
21.	e
22.	h
23.	a
24.	c
25.	g

30.	d
31.	a
32.	c
33.	b
34.	4
35.	1
36.	5
37.	2
38.	3

1. f
2. d
3. e
4. a
5. h
6. j
7. b
8. k
9. g
10. i
11. true
12 false
13. false
14. true
15. false
16. false
17. true
18. true
19. false
20. true
21. b. difficult landing place
22. a a place to worship according to their faith
23. c. stressed syllables
24. a. lullabies and other peaceful poems
25. a. in four-line stanzas
26. b. a ballad
27. b. humor can sometimes get you out of difficulty
28. b. simile
29. a. metaphor
30. c. grass
31. a
32. b
33. b
34. a
35. a
36. A <u>hundred</u> <u>men</u>, as the <u>king</u> heard <u>say</u>.

37. An <u>ancient</u> <u>story</u> I'll <u>tell</u> you a<u>non</u>.
38. <u>Under</u> a <u>spreading</u> <u>chestnut</u> <u>tree</u>.
39. I <u>know</u> that <u>He</u> ab<u>ides</u> with <u>me</u>.
40. I <u>do</u> not <u>know</u> to<u>mor</u>row's <u>way</u>.
41. Examples; any order:
    a. rhythm
    b. rhyme
    c. language
    d. emotion
    e. cadence
    or poetic idea, humor, or poetic devices

ALTERNATE LIFEPAC TEST, Answer Key

1.	3		35.	h
2.	2		36.	a
3.	1		37.	f
4.	2		38.	g
5.	3		39.	F
6.	1		40.	O
7.	b		41.	F
8.	a		42.	O
9.	b		43.	O

10. c
11. a.   Peggy ate too much.
    b.   She feels sick.
12. The tiny, yellow leaves fell off the old tree.
13. Example:
    The blossoming tree stood in the green meadow.
14. Example:
    Kelly raked the leaves up and threw them away.
15. a.   boy
    b.   sandwich
16. c
17. d
18. f
19. i
20. e
21. g
22. h
23. j
24. a
25. b
26. houses
27. goose
28. toys
29. baby
30. foot
31. ladies
32. b
33. d
34. c

1. h
2. b
3. i
4. k
5. g
6. e
7 c
8. d
9 a
10. f
11. false
12 true
13. true
14. false
15. true
16. false
17. true
18. true
19. false
20. true
21. A multitude of people <u>crowded</u> around Jesus.
22. A large boulder <u>tumbled</u> off a cliff.
23. The sidewalk <u>is</u> hot.
24. God <u>is</u> the Creator of the universe.
25. Two white sharks suddenly <u>appeared</u>.

26. regular
27. regular
28. irregular
29. irregular
30. regular
31. irregular
32. irregular
33. regular
34. irregular
35. regular
36. The little boy <u>willingly</u> (offered) his help.
37. The old chest (plunged) <u>quickly</u> to the bottom of the lake.
38. The package will (arrive) <u>later</u>.
39. He did a <u>fairly</u> (good) job for the first time.
40. John (runs) <u>faster</u> than Jason.
41. quicker
42. happily
43. are
44. loudly
45. isn't

1. true
2. false
3. false
4. true
5. false
6. true
7. true
8. false
9. true
10. false
11. a. diagram
12. c. fits his speed to his need
13. a. skim the reading material
14. b. the words explaining a drawing
15. c. scan the article
16. c. outline
17. c. a map
18. b. reads slowly for details
19. b. a chart
20. b. an illustration
21. a diagram
22. read slowly
23. a fact
24. Any order:
    a. charts
    b. diagrams
    c. illustrations
    d. maps
25. a wagon train adventure
26. ten
27. buffalo
28. c. a month
29. b. the prairie grass blow gently in the breeze
30. a. were hunting buffalo
31. a. circled and dug trenches
32. c. burned around the wagon train
33. Herd of buffalo
34. Band of Indians
35. The Prairie Fire

36. Saw smoke in the distance
37. Circled the wagons
38. Kept wagons safe
39. O
40. O
41. F
42. Example:
    My home is painted green.
43. Example:
    My home is the nicest one on the block.

1.	j	42.	cheering
2.	a	43.	ministers'
3.	f	44.	leopard's
4.	c	45.	The cat with the black fur saw the car coming.
5.	i		
6.	b	46.	(")Would you wash the windows(?) (")asked mother(.) (")Sure(,)(") replied Jason(.)
7.	k		
8.	g		
9.	d	47.	N
10.	e	48.	CS
11.	true	49.	CS
12.	true		
13.	false		
14.	true		
15.	false		
16.	false		
17.	true		
18.	true		
19.	false		
20.	true		
21.	c. fable		
22.	a. stress		
23.	a. kinds of humor		
24.	b. free verse		
25.	b. cause and effect		
26.	a. an opinion		
27.	c. speculate or infer		
28.	c. an illustration		
29.	a. dialogue		
30.	b. compare and contrast		
31.	blooming		
32.	was		
33.	green		
34.	The green mountainside		
35.	was blooming with flowers		
36.	broke		
37.	it		
38.	tumbled		
39.	quickly		
40.	triumphantly		
41.	scarcely		